THE SIX HABITS OF HIGHLY CONNECTED PEOPLE

THE SIX HABITS OF HIGHLY CONNECTED PEOPLE

Gerard Kelly

With Ben Wickham

First published 2003 by Spring Harvest Publishing Division and Authentic Lifestyle

09 08 07 06 05 04 03   7 6 5 4 3 2 1

Authentic Lifestyle is an imprint of Authentic media
PO Box 300, Carlisle, Cumbria CA3 0Qs
and PO Box 1047, Waynesboro, GA 30830-2047, USA
www.paternoster-publishing.com

British Library Cataloguing in Publication data

A catalogue record for this book is available from the British Library

1-85078-486-8

Cover design by Diane Bainbridge
Typesetting and illustration by Temple Design
Printed in Great Britain by Bell & Bain Ltd., Glasgow

Contents

FOREWORD

John Archer

It's always annoying when your mobile phone rings in the cinema just as you're about to turn it off. Thankfully the *Gangs of New York* aren't remotely annoyed yet, and I am still being advised that refreshments are available in the foyer. I answer it, deciding to be quick. 'Hi John, it's Ben, look, Gerard and I have written a book and were wondering if you'd write the foreword?' 'Yes of course I will, four words isn't much...' There is a slight pause, 'No John, not four words, a foreword, the beginning of the book.' Now I pause. A huge mobile phone is floating on the screen and the audience in the cinema look ready to act out the first scene of the movie live. 'Yeah sure, e-mail me, bye.' I tell you this just in case some of you are under the illusion that such deals are made at a Christian retreat in an Alpine cottage in Switzerland, between the fondue and coffee.

I've often wondered what a foreword is for. As far as I can see it's like a movie trailer to encourage you to read the book. So maybe this should start with a deep, gravel like, American voice-over,

'Just when you thought it was safe to go out, we bring you... Six Habits.'

Sounds like a horror version of *The Sound of Music*.

No, first let me tell you a little about Gerard Kelly and Ben Wickham. I met them both at Spring Harvest, but at different times; meeting them together would have been too much. They are two very different people. One is young, tall, energetic and good-looking, and the other one is Gerard Kelly. They do have something in common – they are both motivated people.

Together they have come up with a great book. Gerard always makes me think; usually I'm thinking, 'Where did he get that shirt?' This book, however, will make you think a little deeper than his shirt. It will challenge you about who you are, what you do and why you do it.

I read the e-mail proof they sent me, trying to think of how to sum it up and serve as a tasty teaser to you the prospective reader. The following day I had a 'gig' (that's a showbiz word for work). I performed for a church in the Midlands, a pre-Alpha social event. I made them laugh, amazed them with my tricks and then delivered my witty but challenging testimony. Something I have done a thousand times before: that's why I was there, wasn't it? Then at the end of the evening while signing autographs for some children (it's good for my ego) a tiny little girl of about four or five years old wandered up, stood in front of me and held her hands high. I had spotted the girl during the show. She kept leaving her mother to come and stand at the front of the stage and stare at me. An older girl, assuming my ignorance, interpreted the girl's stance for me. 'She wants a hug.' I stared down at the little girl with child protection issues rushing round in my head. She smiled and stretched her hands a little higher. What harm could it do? There were lots of people around. I reached down to pick her up, ready for the SAS to smash through the skylights and pin me to the floor. The little girl grabbed me round the neck and squeezed tight. I looked across the room to see her mother, with big wet eyes, smiling back at me. I put the girl down; she gave me another big smile and ran back to her mother. I packed my props and was about to leave when an older lady came up and spoke to me. 'That little girl you hugged tonight is my next door neighbour, they don't go to church. Her mother wanted me to thank you. Her husband, the little girl's father, died eighteen months ago and you're the first man the little girl has hugged since it happened.' I said, 'Oh, that's nice.' I was numb. I got into the car and drove home through the early hours of the morning. Every now and then my eyes would fill up like that little girl's mother.

That night wasn't about my tricks and jokes, or my cleverly honed testimony. It was about a hug, a hug from God. He hugged me and he hugged that little girl. I thought again about this book. It made sense. That night I was a door. I was plugged in, connected. I felt satisfied; God's mission moved forward and I was blessed. I want to be a pig!

Read the book and you'll understand...

CALLING AT SHEPHERD'S BUSH
The Six Habits of Highly Connected People

> **Creativity is just connecting things. When you ask creative people how they did something, they feel a little guilty because they didn't really do it, they just saw something... they were able to connect experiences they'd had to synthesise new things.** Steve Jobs
>
> It is a sobering fact that nine out of ten people in the world have never made a telephone call in their lives; that despite the propaganda of Bill Gates and other computer salesmen, ninety nine out of every hundred do not have access to the Internet; that Tokyo, with a population of 23 million, has three times as many telephone lines as the whole continent of Africa with 580 million people. Vinoth Ramachandra[1]

Introduction – Invitation to the Dance

Decades after the untimely death of John Lennon, tensions still rage between his widow Yoko Ono and his former business partner Paul McCartney. The latest in a long line of conflicts involves a request by McCartney to change the order in which the two men's names are credited on their songs. Where Lennon/McCartney has been the standard appellation from the start, the surviving partner now wants the songs in which he took a major role to be listed as McCartney/Lennon. The former Mrs Lennon will have none of it, and the rest of us look on and reflect on how sad it is that one of the most creative song-writing partnerships in history should have been so marred by personal differences. Relationships are hard to make and harder to maintain, but most of the good things that have ever come to human history have come through partnership. Think of Gilbert and Sullivan; Bono and The Edge; Fred Astaire and Ginger Rogers. Who would remember Anthony without Cleopatra or watch Laurel without Hardy? Who would laugh at Ant without Dec? Great partnerships are more than the sum of their parts: something is added by their interaction. Individuals may create and inspire, but it is partnerships that make a dent in the universe. Like petrol and sparks, great partnerships ignite.

God's mission – the unfolding adventure of the Creator's love for his creation – is a story of partnership. God does not dance alone, but invites us to join him in a pas-de-deux. He asks us to make *his* mission *our* mission and to share with him the great adventure of redemption. Central to the very nature of mission is that it is made up neither of God's activity alone nor of ours. It is a divine-human partnership. This is not because God cannot act alone, but because he chooses not to. The Creator initiates, but by his choice he draws his creatures into his completion.

> **The life of a candle is neither in the wax nor in the wick, but in the burning.**
> Anon

Noah, Abraham, Moses, Jesus; each was called to step into the spotlight and dance the dance of God for the world's sake. It is when we co-operate with our Creator that life *happens*. Grace, mercy, forgiveness and freedom flow from the heart of God to his broken world, and he asks us to join with him in bringing heaven down to earth. He is the Maker of mercy, but he offers us a share in the distribution contract. He initiates, we deliver.

This book is an exploration of the partnership into which our Maker invites us. At its heart is the metaphor of connection – the idea that just as an appliance can be connected to mains power and a telephone can be connected to its network, so individual humans and the communities they form can 'connect' to the plans and purposes of God.

There is a story told in the computer industry about a call made to one of the early hardware helplines. Informing the harassed helper that his computer wasn't working, the caller was asked, 'What can you see on the screen?'

'There's nothing on the screen,' he replied, after which the conversation went something like this:

'OK, are you sure that the monitor is connected to the CPU?'

'What's the monitor?'

'The part with the screen.'

'What's the CPU?'

'It's the main part of the computer. There should be a lead connecting the two. Is it properly plugged in?'

'I don't know.'

'Why not?'

'Because I can't see it.'

'Why can't you see it?'

'Because the lights have gone out.'

'Can't you switch them on?'

'No, there's been a power cut. The whole building has gone down.'

'Aaaah, I see. Do you still have a receipt for your system and the box it came in?'

'Yes.'

'Right – you need to pack up the machine and take it back to the shop you bought it from.'

'Why, is it really that serious?'

'No, but you need to tell the salesman that you're too darned stupid to own a computer.'

Computers cannot work without power. No matter how high their specification and price tag, no matter what miracles they promise – they will not function until they are *connected*. Even those designed to run on batteries must at some stage be plugged in to be recharged. The same is true of the junk-heap of appliances that fill our homes. We have become so used to electricity that we barely think about it, but our homes are invisibly wired to make connection possible. There is a story from the pre-digital age about a super-confident vacuum-cleaner salesman whose territory included the Highlands of Scotland. Calling on a remote and isolated farmhouse, the Evangelist of the Electrolux strode into the living room to begin his habitual routine. Emptying a bag of dust and dirt onto the carpet, he pointed to his all-singing-all-dancing machine and said 'Madam, if this machine doesn't pick up every speck of this dirt within two minutes, I will eat it myself.' 'I'll fetch ye a spoon,' said the old householder. 'We've nae electricity in the hoose.'

Eastern mystics talk of healthy, effective people as *centred* people: people who have found within themselves the place of peace and harmony from which the peace of the planet can proceed. But history shows us that it is not centred people who change the world but *connected* people: people whose lives are touched by the life of God, who are harnessed to a power beyond themselves and resource their world with the resources of God. Connected lives are infused with the fire of God. Connected people make a difference to their environment because they are a 'point of entry' for grace. The choices they make, the directions they choose, the relationships they make and maintain; all these are shaped and defined by their core connection to God's purposes. They do not contain within themselves the infinite riches of the divine, but they have access to those riches. The lightning of love is God's and God's alone – but connected people are the conductor rods that catch his power for our planet, connecting the life of God to human lives.

Your mission, should you choose to accept it...

The phrase used by theologians to capture the nature and possibility of this connection is Missio Dei – the mission of God. Missio Dei asserts that God himself is at work in our world, seeking those who will work with him for its redemption and rebirth. A broken world is not the last word – God says 'I make all things new', and calls us to join him in *his* core commitment to the winning back of a fallen creation. Missio Dei speaks not only of the power of God but of his purposes, of the love-soaked intentions with which God looks on the cosmos he has created and longs with a full heart for its perfection. This is the central thread running through the Bible, weaving Old and New Testaments together as a panorama of God's unfolding purposes. In *Salvation to the Ends of the Earth*, Andreas J. Köstenberger and Peter T. O'Brien affirm that the mission of God is the key in which the whole narrative of Scripture is written

> ... the divine plan of extending salvation to the ends of the earth is the major thrust of the Scriptures from beginning to end. If the first indications of God's purposes for the world appear in the creation account of Genesis 1, and subsequently in the call of Abram (Gen. 12) which is profoundly related to God's dealings with the nations, then the Bible ends with a vision of 'a great multitude that no-one could count, from every nation, tribe, people and language, standing before the throne and in front of the Lamb' praising in a loud voice and saying, 'Salvation belongs to our God, who sits on the throne, and to the Lamb' (Rev. 7:9-10; cf. 14:6). God's saving plan for the whole world forms a grand frame around the entire story of Scripture.[2]

It is with the mission of God that we connect because it is the mission of God that most fully expresses his intentions and interests.

> **The church does not define its mission. God does. It is God's mission in the world that concocts the church, not the other way around.**
>
> Leonard Sweet[3]

I want to be a door...

There is a scene in *Monsters Inc.* in which a small band of reluctant heroes – two scary monsters and a small child – find themselves in the overlap between two worlds. Before them an array of bedroom doors are suspended on a complex system of cogs and conveyor belts: a million hanging hunks of hardware clanking and clicking through a never-ending dance-of-the-doors. Red doors and blue doors; old doors and new doors; scratched and tatty doors with children's names on; doors intricately painted with decals and daisies. Door after door flies by in a blur of bedrooms. But this is no DIY warehouse. These doors are more than stock for the shelves of B&Q. Each different door is a portal, a point-of-entry, into the human sphere. The rooms beyond these doors – every one of them the bedroom of a child – are the landing places on which the visions that scare meet the victims who scream. The doors are inter-dimensional, every one a connection between two worlds.

I WANT TO BE A DOOR

Find a quiet place where you can do some imagining without being disturbed. Relax. Picture yourself standing in front of a door. For the moment, it is a closed door. What does it look like? Is it decorated or plain? Is it an interior or an exterior door? Now imagine that this is a meeting point between the kingdom of heaven and the world in which you live. You are standing on God's side of the door, waiting to connect with the world. The door in question is you: your life; your gifts and skills; your dreams. God is trying to connect with the creation through you.

Now open the door.

Who is there? What environment does it open into? Who and what can God connect with through you?

This chaotic and colourful scene is a wonderful picture of the workings of the kingdom of God. Somewhere, in a realm beyond our own, the plans of God are formulated and rolled out, promising blessings for the earth. On our side of the deal, a world of need cries out for these same blessings. Between the two – linking two worlds and making the mission of God possible – there are *connected* people. In *Monsters Inc.* it is doors that bridge two worlds: in the kingdom of God it is people. The infinite ocean of the mercies of God becomes a cup of water to the thirsty soul because it passes through the pipes and taps of connected people. It is through connected people that God's mission comes in to land. And landing the mission of God – bringing heaven down to earth – is the central vocation of the Christian disciple. The call to follow Christ is a call to connect.

Created, called, connected

The more you explore the concept of the 'mission of God' – the more you journey with the many people in our churches seeking to clarify their role in that mission – the more you will see that 'connection' is the central metaphor of Christian calling. No habit is higher and no aim more admirable than the quest to connect with God's mission. The greatest missionary endeavours in the world will count for nothing if they don't connect with the mission of God, but the smallest acts of kindness are magnified beyond measure when they do. The most powerful passion will prove destructive unless it is connected to God's passion. The highest purpose will not produce life unless it is connected to God's purposes. Unconnected, millions can be given and spent to no avail. Connected, the widow's merest mite can touch heaven and change the earth.

Like a *Cable Guy*'s dream come true, the world is awash with people waiting for connection. Connection is at one and the same time the call, the content, the fruit and the fulfilment of God's mission. If you are seeking to live your life as a follower of Jesus, connection matters because:

■ *Connection* is mission. Our missionary God is already at work in our world, asking each of us only to find our place and purpose in his plans. We are tiny vessels hoarding water by the thimbleful: he is a vast lake of potential, enough for all with more to spare. The sheer scale of the contrast between God's assets and ours; between the majestic span of his purposes and the chicken-scratchings of ours; between the sweeping breadth of his field of vision and the tunnel-blindness of ours, should be enough to convince us of the need for connection. Unconnected we stumble blindly like children trying to pin the tail of mission to the donkey of the world's need. Connected, we are guided and empowered.

■ *Connection* is for each of us – young and old, ordained and lay, 'full-time' and 'no-time'. There are as many connections to God's mission as there are human beings to connect. Every door is different, and there is a door with your name on it. The combination of atoms and attributes that is represented by the word YOU has never existed before and never will again. The experiences that have shaped you like waves sculpting driftwood have not produced the exact same contours anywhere else in time or space. Even though the atoms of your anatomy have played a part in other bodies before you; even though the air you breathe is borrowed; even though your every molecule is second-hand: still you are a one-off. The you that is you has never been you before. And the place God has for you in his purposes is similarly unique. No two tigers have exactly the same stripes – and no two Christians have the same call.

■ *Connection* is the key. Many followers of Jesus spend years plagued by questions of direction and guidance. Should I serve God 'full-time', or develop a career? Should I go abroad or stay at home? Am I called to evangelism or to social action? Is my arena the church or the world beyond the church's doors? Should I work with drug addicts, write to my MP, promote fairly-traded coffee, write poetry or spend time with friends at the pub? Should I pray more and do less, or do more and pray while I'm doing it? Our understanding of mission is shaped by duty, guilt and need and none of these is ever satisfied. Unless we can answer the deeper question: 'How do I *connect* with God's mission?' we will always be the victims of unreachable goals. Once we know we are connecting, other questions lose their power and the vicious circle is tamed. Connecting with God's mission is the first and last priority of our lives.

There are many questions you can ask about a telephone.

Does it have automatic redial?

Is there a number to press for an outside line?

Will it work on speakerphone?

But there is only one question that matters.

Is it connected?

Connecting your call

But how do we connect? How can each follower of Jesus identify that unique calling for which they were created? How do you find the door to your particular bedroom? We have found six clues to this mystery hidden in the life and call of Moses: the burnt-out shepherd called through a burning bush. Recorded in the early chapters of the book of Exodus, the calling of Moses offers a remarkable window into the possibility of connecting with God's mission.

'I have not failed,' Thomas Edison once wrote, 'I have just found ten thousand ways that won't work.' Moses would probably not have made such a distinction. Failing was exactly what he had done. Confused in both identity and destiny, he was disappointed, depressed and disillusioned – so much so that he gave his first son a name that in essence means 'Exile'. The timeline of his life ran at a steep angle downwards. From a spectacular start involving miracles, million-to-one chances and immeasurable power and privilege, he had come to an eighty-year mid-point of ordinariness, obscurity, failure and frustration. He had tried to force the purposes of God by his own hand and had fallen hard. Rejected both by his blood clan and by his adopted family, he had single-handedly managed to offend just about everyone in the circles of his life. The Exodus narrative doesn't tell us explicitly that he was ready to give up, but its implicit message is that he

already had. A measure of potential unprecedented among the Hebrew slaves had been poured down the drain of personal dysfunction.

Picture for a moment the inflatable boy enrolled in an inflatable school with an inflatable teacher. On the day he took a sharp pin to school, his teacher sternly told him – 'Not only have you let the school down, but you've let me down and, worst of all, you've let yourself down.' This was Moses: a bouncy castle with the air let out. If Moses were a bank account, he would be in the red and close to foreclosure. If he were a car he would be immobile, with little chance of a clean MOT without cheating. If he were on sale in a supermarket, he would be reduced to clear.

> Years had passed since Moses had fled from Egypt. He was living a pastoral life, looking after Jethro's sheep in the lonely pastureland under the shadow of Mount Horeb. Here were the simple conditions of revelation: a man in solitude, with openness of heart, having retreated from the pomp and politics of Egyptian society. The place was right, the time was right, the man was right. And suddenly Moses caught sight of the common bush aflame with God.
>
> Brother Ramon SSF[4]

The call of God turned Moses around. Something happened to the old shepherd, beginning with the sight of a burning bush on the mountainside at Horeb, that changed everything. He connected with God's mission and was transformed. Disconnected, he had succeeded only in bringing trouble on his family and friends. Connected to God's mission, the most powerful dictatorship in the world could not defeat him. There are six keys that emerge in the narrative of Moses' call that identify six distinct elements of connection:

■ PASSION

Moses finds a connection between the deepest passions of his heart and the passion in the heart of God.

■ PLACE

Moses makes a connection *in* the place in which God calls him *for* the place to which he is called.

■ PURPOSE

Moses discovers the connection between the evident purposes of his own life and the purposes of God for his context and culture.

■ POWER

Moses connects his strengths and his weaknesses to the power of God, and finds transformation in both.

■ PROCESS

Moses finds a connection with the process and pace by which God has worked, is working and will work in his life.

■ PERSPECTIVE

Moses connects his own role in the mission of God to the wider perspective of history, finding his place in God's promise-plan.

These are the six 'pins' of connection to God's mission, and from them emerge the six habits of highly connected people. Exploring these six will offer many opportunities to re-configure our own lives. By connecting in each, we will build towards a whole-life connection to God's mission. *Connection* is a win-win proposition. As we come into line with God's purposes and find our unique place in his plans:

– We inherit a measure of life-satisfaction unheard of in any other sphere

– God's mission moves forward by a few precious steps

– Those we have been set apart to serve receive the blessings God has set aside for them.

There are no losers in this deal – connection is a doorway to life both for those who step through it and for those they touch in the process. This comes close to explaining one of Jesus' favourite riddles, recorded in Matthew 10:39: 'Whoever finds his life will lose it, and whoever loses his life for my sake will find it.' In the kingdom of God, you win by losing. Connecting to God's mission is the only way you can spend everything you've got and still make a profit; the only sphere in which you find yourself by giving yourself away. It's like buying a lottery ticket every day of your life, never coming up in the winning numbers and yet knowing, as deeply as it is possible to know, that you are a winner.

Psychiatrist M. Scott Peck tells the story of a woman he was treating on a regular basis. She was comfortably off and in many ways successful, but wrestled with a range of problems that amounted to clinical depression. On one occasion she was late for her appointment, but was also visibly different. Normally distracted and unfocused, she was instead motivated, animated and alive. Scott Peck remarked on this and asked her if she knew why it might be. His patient explained that her car had failed to start that morning, and she had asked her neighbour, a clergyman, for a lift into town to meet her appointment. The neighbour agreed to take her, but mentioned that he had to make a stop on the way to visit some members of his congregation who were in hospital – and that she would have to come with him. She did so, and found herself drawn into conversation with some of the patients. As she explained to Scott Peck, spending time with people whose circumstances were so much worse than her own, being able to help them just by listening, had put her own problems into perspective and lifted her spirits. Scott Peck pointed her to the obvious conclusion. 'This has clearly helped you a lot,' he said, 'so why not use it as therapy? Don't come and see me every week – go and see them instead.' She looked at him with an expression of total horror and exclaimed, 'You don't expect to do *that* every week, do you?'

What this patient failed to see is that connecting with God's mission – 'spending yourself', as Isaiah 58 puts it, 'on behalf of the poor', is an *energising* connection. Service is a source of strength and healing. A connection to God's mission is a connection to life.

Definition: SERVOPHOBIA – fear of doing what we know will make us happy because logic and the propaganda of the marketplace tell us that it won't.

Charles De Foucauld was the son of a wealthy family in nineteenth century France. An officer in the army, his early adult years were lived entirely for selfish gain in a rejection of the Catholicism of his childhood. A radical conversion experience changed everything, and De Foucauld became 'Brother Charles', living out his days in the deserts of North Africa as a monk and hermit. He prayed, served the poor and sought to imitate 'the hidden life of Jesus'. 'When one is very sure that something is the will of God,' he wrote in his journal, 'it is so sweet to do the will of the Beloved that nothing else counts. He is here as he was at Nazareth. He is everywhere. What does it matter where I am? One thing only matters and that is to be where he wishes me to be, to do what pleases him most. Oh let us forget ourselves, forget ourselves, and live in Jesus, loving him with all our hearts; for you know when one loves one lives less for oneself than for the Beloved, and the more one loves the more one directs one's life towards him whom one loves.'

If your experience, like that of Moses, is less an overnight success story and more a life-long struggle to connect, take some time to consider the potential for change. Ask God what bushes he might burn to get your attention, to speak into your life and to turn you around. Create space – for reflection, redirection and renewal. Open up to the remarkable possibilities of a connected life. You may find it helpful to pray this prayer, written by David Adam for the context of a busy working life:

The Furnace of God's Love

Lord, I am poured out,
I come to you for renewal.
Lord, I am weary,
I come to you for refreshment.
Lord, I am worn,
I come to you for restoration.
Lord, I am lost,
I come to you for guidance.
Lord, I am troubled,
I come to you for peace.
Lord, I am lonely,
I come to you for love.
Come, Lord,
Come revive me
Come re-shape me
Come mould me in your image.
Re-cast me in the furnace of your love.

David Adam[5]

Six and out

As we sketch out and explore the possibilities of a more connected life, the six 'pins' identified above offer signposts for the journey. Each will take you to a different aspect of your life and circumstances, asking you in a variety of ways to observe the landscape in which you find yourself and the self you find. Each of the six has been expressed as a life-commitment or habit – creating the Six Habits of Highly Connected People. This reflects the reality that none of this is the work of a moment. These are ongoing choices that may need to be made again and again. There is a popular illusion amongst the followers of Jesus that 'connection' happens in early life and is good for the duration. This leads some to see it as too easy and others to believe that it's too late – that if you miss the early bus there is no later service. The truth is that this is a project of a lifetime. There is no 'crash diet' or 'detox plan' that can set your life on the right track once and for all – you need a long-term change of attitude and lifestyle. Moments of change can have value and purpose, but it is habits of change that will transform you. Connection with the mission of God is like a healthy diet – it's never too early to get the habit, and never too late to get it back.

> **In theory there is no difference between theory and practice. But in practise there is.**
>
> Jan L. A. Van de Snepscheut

The Taming of the Truth

Like a football match
Where the fans are locked out
While the players take turns
On the terraces
To cheer.

Like a concert
Where the crowd sit in silence
While the band play
Through headphones
So that only they hear.

Like a hospital that keeps itself
Germ-free and sterile
By only treating patients
Who aren't sick.

Like a spoonful of sugar
With no medicine.
Like a mule
Without a kick.

Like an ocean liner
On a pleasure cruise
Purely for the pleasure
Of the crew.

We have taken
What was given
As a message for the many
And made of it
A massage
For the few.

Gerard Kelly

F – U – N – E – M – N – X?

As you give each of the six habits the attention it needs, and begin to bring the six together, you will find a pattern emerging of a life re-oriented towards the purposes of God. It may take some time for a clear picture to emerge, and there may be clouds and obstacles to get through on the way, but there are fruits to be won for those prepared to press through. The journey into connection with God's mission is for many a journey from involvement to commitment. Millions of people the world over are 'involved' in Christianity, but the truly committed are fewer and harder to find. Connection moves you from passive to active service: it is a call to commitment. Like the chicken and the pig walking across the farmyard discussing the politics of bacon and eggs, you need to know the difference between involvement and commitment. (The chicken is involved – the pig is committed.)

PIGS AND CHICKENS

On a large piece of paper, write a word or phrase to represent each of the activities or commitments that fill your life. You can express these in terms of 'roles' if that seems the easiest way – for instance 'husband' or 'wife', 'amateur actor', 'Sunday school teacher', 'hairdresser' etc. Try to include all the things you regularly commit time to, including clubs, associations, hobbies and leisure pursuits.

Now write or draw against each of these to designate 'pig' or 'chicken'. 'Pig' goes against the things you are genuinely committed to – I would die for this. 'Chicken' goes against things you are involved in, but could live without – I definitely would not die for this.

Reflect on what you now see. Are your 'pigs' the things you thought they would be? Do you have too many 'chickens'? What would it take for you to redirect resources and energy from the 'chickens' to the 'pigs'?

The invitation at the heart of this book is a little unusual, but it is real nonetheless: make the journey from eggs to bacon – from involvement to commitment – by connecting with the mission of God. Don't be a chicken – be a pig.

References

1 Vinoth Ramachandra, *Faiths in Conflict? Christian Integrity in a multi-cultural world*, (IVP: 2000) p9

2 Andreas J. Köstenberger and Peter T. O'Brien, *Salvation to the Ends of the Earth: a biblical theology of mission*, (IVP: 2001) p262

3 Leonard Sweet, *Carpe Manana*, (Zondervan: 2001)

4 Brother Ramon SSF, *Deeper Into God* (Zondervan, 1987), p24

5 David Adam, *Power Lines* (Triangle SPCK, 1992)

- **PASSION** – I will seek a connection between the deepest passions of my heart and the passion in the heart of God.

- **PLACE** – I will seek to connect with God *in* the place in which I stand, *for* the place to which he is calling me.

- **PURPOSE** – I will look for the connection between the evident purposes of my own life and the purposes of God for my context and culture.

- **POWER** – I will seek to connect my strengths and my weaknesses to the power of God, and seek his transformation in both.

- **PROCESS** – I will connect with the process and pace by which God has worked, is working and will work in my life.

- **PERSPECTIVE** – I will look for the connection between my role in the mission of God and the wider perspective of history, finding my place in God's promise-plan.

PASSION

Habit #1– I will seek a connection between the deepest passions of my heart and the passion in the heart of God

> The best argument for Christianity is Christians; their joy, their certainty, their completeness. But the strongest argument *against* Christianity is also Christians – when they are sombre and joyless, when they are self-righteous and smug in complacent consecration, when they are narrow and repressive, then Christianity dies a thousand deaths. Sheldon Vanauken[1]
>
> A prominent Hindu once said that he would believe in the Christian Saviour if Christians only looked a little more saved. Anon

The closest I have ever come to being the subject of a citizen's arrest was in a branch of my bank. It was the pre-Christmas season, following the birth of my youngest son, Jacob. We were on a family shopping trip to the Merry Hill Centre, one of Britain's most sacred temples of consumer culture. We split up – Chrissie went to look for presents while I visited the bank. I paid in some cheques and was heading back through the mall to meet Chrissie, when I was stopped by an announcement over the tannoy system. 'Will Mr Gerard Kelly please return to the Nationwide Building Society.' I immediately began to think what I might have left at the bank. I checked my pockets to see that I had my chequebook with me. I checked my wallet to see that I had my cards. I checked my recall to see that I hadn't left anything else.

I couldn't think why they had called me back, and began to wonder if they had looked into my bulging overdraft and were out to get me.

As I arrived at the branch four uniformed members of staff looked up in unison. The manageress addressed me. 'It's all right,' she said, 'he's here.' Confirming, in their eyes, my utter depravity, I asked the wrong question. 'Who's here?' It was at this moment that I followed their gaze to the back office where I could just make out a familiar-looking pushchair and my five-month-old son entertaining two more members of staff. I had left the baby in the bank.

As I gathered my wits, mumbled my thanks and apologies and quickly pushed a smiling Jake back out into the mall, I felt six pairs of eyes drilling into me. I glanced back once to catch a look on the face of the manageress that was the closest I have ever seen to a phone call to Social Services. Jacob seemed unfazed by the interlude, and has not to my knowledge developed an irrational fear either of banks or of women in uniform – but it goes without saying that I now pay in my cheques elsewhere.

In forgetting my son, if only for a moment, I had stepped into a territory on which God has never walked. The core of the revelation of Yahweh at the burning bush, the fact that overwhelms all others and utterly changes the way Moses sees the world, is the fact that God does not forget. The scene is set by the closing words of Exodus Chapter 2:

> EX. 2:23 During that long period, the king of Egypt died. The Israelites groaned in their slavery and cried out, and their cry for help because of their slavery went up to God. 24God heard their groaning and he remembered his covenant with Abraham, with Isaac and with Jacob. 25So God looked on the Israelites and was concerned about them.

Scholars note that these words ascribe four active verbs to God: God hears, God remembers, God sees and God knows (is concerned). The God whom Moses is about to encounter is neither passive nor pitiless, neither unfeeling nor uncon-

cerned. Though the Hebrew people may have thought him silent for four hundred years, though Moses may have wondered if he cared, God has heard and seen the plight of the slaves. He has forgotten neither his people nor his promises. Moved by their sufferings, he is determined to act for their freedom. Moses discovers that there is passion surging in the heart of God. As Philip Greenslade has written

> The God of our story is not woodenly acting out a pre-determined script. He is living out a passion for his people and for the world's redemption ... This is a God who is passionately aroused by injustice, and plunges into emotional involvement with his people ... God hears and feels, sees and knows, remembers and acts to save his people.[2]

The narrative shows Moses 'connecting' with the passion of God in three distinct phases: recognition, response and redirection.

Recognition – God's passion is the foundation

Moses' first step into his call lies in recognising the passion of God. It is because God cares – not because we care – that mission exists. Whatever our particular calling is, it will be grounded in God's great passion, the cornerstone of all Christian mission. In both content and

GOD HAS REMEMBERED

Props – a recent copy of a daily or weekly newspaper and a thick red felt-tipped pen.

Take a recent edition of a daily or weekly newspaper. Spread it out on a desk or table, or on the floor. Look at the pictures, headlines and main articles, and against each ask these two questions:

'Who is there in this story who might think that God has forgotten them? What is the cry of the human heart behind this story?'

Wherever you find an individual or group who might not know that God has heard their cry and remembered their need, use the marker to circle their name or image. Then take some time to pray for each one, and ask yourself 'through whom will God connect with each of these people?'

strength, God's passion is our model and our marker. Christian service is never a solo performance – it is a partnership between caller and called, between the God who cares more than we can even begin to and we who have begun to care.

> God hears and feels, sees and knows, remembers and acts to save his people.
>
> Philip Greenslade and Selwyn Hughes[3]

We cannot take the needs of the whole world onto our shoulders – and it is clear that God will not ask us to do so. But whatever he does ask us to do, whatever part we are given to play, it will reflect these four principles – God has heard and remembered, seen and known.

If even this is still unclear to you – if you do not yet sense the stirrings of the passion of God, begin a season of seeking. Through prayer and openness, ask God to open your ears to the cries you haven't heard and your eyes to the pain you haven't seen and ask him to reveal to you something of the passion he feels. Don't look yet for instructions or objectives – your first goal, pure and simple, is to feel the passion. Stop. Listen. What do you hear?

> The wonder of the narrative is that the cry from below evoked the power of God from above. In response to the slave cry, God moved the darkness and the sea, God mobilised creation on behalf of the needy slaves, God managed the chaos redemptively. They were freed, as they never expected to be!
>
> Walter Brueggemann[4]

The miracle of the Exodus narrative is that a connection is made between the pain of the slaves and the passion of God. There is no indication that the cry of the slaves was any more than a cry of desperation. Did they know that God would hear, or was their anguish sent out into an empty universe marked 'To whom it may concern?' Did they feel that their prayers were bouncing off the ceiling? Whether they did or not, the reality is that God heard. A connection was made between the condition of the people and the concern of their God. The cry of torment on its way up through the heavens met the love of God on its way down.

Response – God's passion inspires my participation

The second phase in Moses' experience of God's call was the phase of response – he had to 'catch' the passion of God for himself. Os Guinness, in The Call, writes, 'God's calling is the key to igniting a passion for the deepest growth and highest heroism in life. But search as you will, there is no higher or more ultimate passion than a human being ablaze with a desire for God.'[5]

The evidence that the passion has been caught – that something of the surging strength of God's heart has crossed over into that of Moses – is seen in the continuing story of life beyond the burning bush. As the adventure unfolds,

Moses finds that he must communicate all that God has done and said: first to Aaron, then to the elders of Israel, then to all the people. In each case his passion builds. It becomes clear that he has identified with the plans and purposes of God: that the passion of God has somehow been transmitted. The acid test comes when the Hebrew slaves finally hit the Red Sea – the boundary that will mark either the end of their slavery or the end of their lives. They are tired, fearful, disgruntled, confused and hungry, and the tooled-up commandos of the Egyptian army are bearing down on them. Six hundred of Pharaoh's crack troops have leapt into their chariots – the fighter jets of their day – and are heading into battle, ready to kill. The slaves' complaint to Moses is stark and graphic: 'Was it because there were no graves in Egypt that you brought us to the desert to die?' (Ex. 14:11).

Moses faces the prospect that his new job as the de facto leader of Israel may be short-lived. Has he freed the slaves only to make their situation and his own worse? Is this the end of the line for God's promise? But something has happened to the doubting Moses. The man who questioned every word of God's call to him, whose life was dominated not by faith but by fear, has changed. The passion of God has so infused his consciousness, so changed his ways of thinking that he is able to say with confidence: 'Do not be afraid. Stand firm and you will see the deliverance the LORD will bring you today. The Egyptians you see today you will never see again. The LORD will fight for you; you need only to be still' (Ex. 14:13,14).

> **Faith is something you are ready to die for. Doctrine is something you're prepared to kill for. There is a world of difference between the two.**
>
> Tony Benn

God's passion has become Moses' passion, and with it have come confidence, direction and strength. Moses recognises a passion in the heart of God that is so deep and unchanging that there is no longer room for doubt. If God cares this much, then surely he will act for us. The first step towards making God's goals our goals is to make God's passion our passion. As we come to care about the things God cares about, we will find ourselves drawn into the actions that flow from his care: passion will translate into priorities. The more deeply we feel as God feels, the more fluently we will act as God acts. If the mission of God is a river that runs through history and into our lives, then the passion of God is its source. Connect to the source, and you will find yourself moving with the river.

Redirection – God's passion remoulds my own

Lastly, it is significant that Moses' life was not without its passions before the call of God came. We are told little of his early adult life, but three key incidents are recorded to show how deeply a passion for justice ran in his veins. He intervenes in an incident between an Egyptian and a Hebrew (Ex. 2:11), then again in a conflict between two slaves (Ex. 2:13). These actions backfire and he runs from Egypt into neighbouring Midian. The first thing he does on arrival is to intervene again, rescuing Jethro's daughters from the unwanted attention of the local shepherds (Ex. 2:17). What kind of portrait is painted of Moses if the three incidents recorded from his early adult life all show him intervening to deal with a perceived injustice? Given that this is all we are told about these years, we can safely surmise that he was a passionate, impetuous man.

> **What will you wish you'd done before you died? Paint a self-portrait? Build a house? Don't wait until it's too late. Do it now. Otherwise your last thought on this planet will be regret.**
>
> *Fight Club*

The passion with which Moses would later confront Pharaoh, lead the slaves to freedom and shape the nation of Israel is not solely received at the burning bush – it is also a redemption and redirection of his own, God-given passions. The seeds of what Moses will become are present already in his early years. But without the intervention of God these are unchannelled, untamed passions. Their object is right and their depth admirable, but they lead only to destruction.

MEMORY-MARKERS

Find a quiet place where you are free to do some thinking without being disturbed. Bring to mind times and incidents in your life when you have felt a deep connection to the passion of God. These might include activities you have been involved in or relationships that have been important to you. Try to identify three or four of these memories, then ask yourself: what do they have in common? What do these activities or incidents tell me about my own motivations and passions?

God must take these raw materials – the fuel and oxygen that will later blaze – and redirect them to his purposes. Moses not only learns how to see and embrace the passion of God, but also how to know, control and direct his own passions. The mission of God does not negate the strong feelings he has been plagued with all his life: but it gives to them a legitimate goal, a constructive course and a manageable current.

Definition: WHATEVER – a word that, used as a sentence in its own right, has no part in God's vocabulary.

Moses makes a strong and lasting connection between the deepest passions of his own heart and the passion he has found in the heart of God. You can connect with the mission of God for your life by recognising his passion as the foundation of all mission; by allowing your own goals and priorities to be shaped by his passion; by asking him to redirect and redeem your own deepest passions. Mission without passion is like a surfer without waves – the board may look impressive, but there is no life in it.

Connection begins in the surging surf of the passion of God.

Inspiration or indifference?

'Parallel Universe' was an alternative worship service that met for some years at Cityside Baptist Church in Auckland, New Zealand. One of their services centred on the idea of fire as an image of God's passion, and included a meditation called 'Fire in the Dark'.

Burning with passion.
On fire with desire.
Flaming with fervour.
The fire of God has fallen.
The fire is on our heads, in our hearts, in our guts.
Ripping through the paper walls of apathy, popping the windows of reserve,
consuming the frames of indifference.
The fire is in our blood, in our arteries, in our brains, pumping through our bodies.

When the fire falls,
there is blazing heat and light.
Here there is darkness.
Where the fire falls,
there is passion and zeal and
abandon.
Where the fire falls,
there is life and love and passion.
Come down, fire of God.
Fall on us, fire of God.
Kindle the flame, fire of God.
Burn us and brand us
and inflame us and consume us.
Set us ablaze so we flare and roar.
Intensity. Ardour. Rapture.
Burning with life.
The word of the Lord is a fire in my
heart
and a hammer in my bones.
May the fire embrace us.
May the fire deliver us.
May the fire purify us.
May the fire enliven us.
May the fire roar.
May the fire spread.
Fire of God we welcome you.

Mike Riddell[6]

In stark contrast, Douglas Coupland captures the malaise of those in our culture who find they are less passionate than they have ever been – for whom the overwhelming stimulus of a culture on sensory overdrive produces not passion but apathy.

> Here's what was on my mind: I have recently begun worrying about my feelings disappearing more and more – noticing that I had less... I was wondering what was the logical end product of this business of my feeling less and less. Is feeling nothing the inevitable end result of believing nothing? And then I got to feeling frightened – thinking that there might not actually be anything to believe in, in particular. I thought it would be a sick joke to have to remain alive for decades and not believe in or feel anything.[7]

As you read these two passages, which most strongly echoes your own life? Which is closer to your own experience? If you resonate more deeply with Coupland than Riddell, what paths might be open to you to move from apathy to passion? These are real and relevant questions in a world in which experience has largely been 'virtualised', so that strength of feeling is a commodity to be consumed like tomato soup or aspirin: divorced from events in the everyday world. This manufacturing of passion has two equal and opposite effects. It heightens and intensifies the way we experience passion: raising expectations and building compulsions, but at the same time it reduces and weakens our capacity to connect with real passions. So we have more video games and less real challenges; more sexual experiences and less love; more magic moments and less purpose.

PASSION-METER

Take a blank sheet of paper and note on it the things you think you are passionate about. What are the activities or aspects of your life that connect with the deepest passions of your heart? Leave some space against each item.

Alongside these, record the things you do but about which you are not entirely passionate. This can include things you hate doing (cleaning toilets is rarely a high spot of personal passion) or things you do 'in neutral' (like a job you tolerate but are not inspired by). Leave space against each item.

Now reflect on the amount of time you have committed to them in the past week, month, quarter or year. You will have to decide what an appropriate timeframe is for your situation and based on the information you have to hand. If you have measurable information, note the total time commitment next to each item.

Think about your results. Are you struggling to make time for the things you care about? Is there anything you can do to change this? Is it possible, in your circumstances, for your time to more fully reflect your passion? What does this exercise tell you about how your life is, how it could be and how it should be?

Definition: COMFORT ZONER – a person who stays within the boundaries of a familiar lifestyle and experience, and struggles to break out. Symptoms include a reluctance to try new things, see new places or meet new people.

Real passion, by contrast, is connected to real events and offers real outcomes. It deals with substance and draws us into action. It is a passion that does not destroy, but rather feeds us. Just as the bush that caught Moses' attention was 'on fire but did not burn up', so the passion of God will inspire and inflame without devouring us. God's passion is the one connection we can make that allows us to burn without burnout.

Lord grant me ... that my lamp may feel thy kindling touch and know no quenching; may burn for me and, for others, may give light.

Prayer of Columbanus

Into the fire

It is a key message of the Exodus narrative that God calls us to run into his passion, not away from it. The fires of passion burn hot, and we are not averse to pulling back from it. Passion is disruptive and dangerous. We fear its impact and its effects. We fear for our reputation – that we will be called irrational fanatics or, in the single most frequent misuse of language developed in the twentieth century, fundamentalists. Better to stay cool and unmoved, in the safe places where the fire does not fall. But if the fire we fear is God's fire, we are wrong to hold back. The road to fulfilment is obedience. There are times in our lives when the only route open to us is through the fire.

Definition: AGGROPHOBIA – the fear of making major life changes on the grounds that other people might be upset. Often focused on colleagues at work, immediate neighbours or your mother-in-law.

Forest fires are a regular occurrence in Australia and they are hugely destructive, killing thousands of animals and destroying vast swathes of the bush. The force and direction of a fire is guided by the wind. Where the wind blows, the fire burns. The faster the wind, the faster the flames rush across the bush, destroying everything in their path. When a fire is moving at full speed across the landscape, not even kangaroos can outrun the flame tide. The only animal that survives the Australian bush fires is the dingo. Instead of running from the fast-advancing heat wall, these wild dogs turn and face the fire. They crouch down low and wait. Their every muscle tense, their eye focusing on the blaze ahead of them, they bide their time as the flames approach. Not until the leading edge of the fire is inches from their nose do they act, springing forwarded to leap through the flames. Some will be injured in the jump – their nose a little burnt, their fur singed but as often as not they land safely on the smoking ground behind the waves of fire. The way forward is not to run from the fire, but to pass through it.

God sends his fire to inspire us, but also to purify and change us. There are things about ourselves that we will only see by the light of his fire as it burns. We walk a tightrope between extremes – on the one hand of a passion so out of control that we lose touch with reality; on the other coldness so extreme that nothing moves us. Somewhere in between these two is a place where the fire of God, life-giving and inspiring, meets and changes us. The key to steering clear of both extremes is to seek the strongest possible connection between our own passions and the passion of God. This calls for two parallel movements – towards greater self-knowledge and towards the knowledge of God. Growth in Christian discipleship is never about only one of these, and always about both. The more you know of God, the more accurately and confidently you will be able

---

WHAT IS YOUR PASSION? PART 1

Pick up today's newspaper and flick through the pages. What are the first two articles you read?

to recognise, understand and appreciate his passion. And the more you see of yourself by his light, the more discerning you will be of the roots of your own passions. As you come to know God more fully and to know yourself more clearly, you will see your passions coming more and more into line with God's heart. When you burn hot, it will be for good reason.

Three further principles emerge from the Exodus narrative that mark out the contours of the passion of God and may help you to sharpen your capacity to see and understand the heart of God.

1 God is watching

We can perhaps begin to imagine how Moses felt about the four hundred years in which God seemed unmoved by the worsening plight of the Hebrew slaves. The silence of God is one of the most painful things we are asked as human beings to endure and Moses had experienced more than his share of it. He must have been tempted, as we so often are, to believe that God had not seen the situation his people were facing. Better to think of God as blind rather than as cruel in his indifference. But the discovery Moses makes is that God is watching. He has seen the plight of his people. He has witnessed every blow struck against them. He has been present with them, watching over them in love, preparing for the moment of intervention. It is a core credal statement of faith in Yahweh that God *sees*. Nothing is hidden from him, and no event befalls us – for good or ill – that he does not know.

For Moses, this is good news – but it is not always so. For the oppressed and abused, the phrase 'God sees' is a statement of hope. For the oppressor, it brings judgement. The story is told of a man who, with great regularity, would drink himself into a drunken stupor at a neighbourhood bar and then stagger home, to the dismay of his wife. One night, he came home thoroughly drunk and vomited all over the kitchen floor. His wife decided she had had enough. She called the pastor of her church, who quickly came over to deal with this situation. They carried the drunken man upstairs and tucked him into bed. Then the pastor prayed over him, saying 'Dear Lord, as you look upon this vomiting drunk...' The man interrupted the pastor, and with slurred speech, said, 'Don't tell him I'm drunk! Tell him I'm sick!'

For this man, the thought that God sees all is no comfort – he would rather be hidden than seen; unknown than known. We come to God on our terms, mentally noting all the things we hope he has missed. But there are none. His terms involve total honesty – we are transparent before him.

In the convent school dining room a bowl of fresh, juicy apples had been placed on the servery table. Beside them, Mother Superior had left a hand-written note saying: 'Take only one – remember,

God is watching.' At the other end of the table was a tray of freshly baked chocolate chip cookies. Beside these a hastily scrawled note, in a child's handwriting, said: 'Take all you want – God's watching the apples.'

God's vision is not split nor his attention divided. Our faith begins in the certain knowledge that he sees and knows all there is to be seen and known about us. Whether we receive this as good news or bad will depend on whether we are proud or ashamed of our lives. For most of us there will be a mixture of the two. The greater truth is that God's knowledge of us, no matter what the content of our lives, is our security – because we can fall upon his overwhelming love and mercy and because we need not fear some future discovery that will make him regret his trust in us. If there are skeletons in your cupboard, you can be sure that God has seen them, has counted their every bone, and has no fear of them. God will constantly surprise you with his grace – you will never surprise him with your secrets. A god who loved you because he didn't know the truth would be no god worth knowing. The miracle of Yahweh is that he sees and knows all, yet still loves you.

2 Love is listening

Central to Moses' call is the affirmation that God has heard his people's cry. This is presented more as a cry of pain than a thought-through and God-directed prayer. We are told that the Israelites

> **THE REALITY OF SILENCE**
>
> Find an undisturbed space and sit in silence for five solid minutes. Try to calm your thoughts until the silence is real. Resist the temptation to pray. Once you have established a true silence, ask yourself, 'What do I hear?'

'groaned in their slavery and cried out, and their cry for help because of their slavery went up to God' (Ex. 2:23). The implication is not that the slaves organised a national call to prayer, but that they were in pain, and in their pain cried out. This is not a prayer of faith but of desperation, directed towards anyone who is listening. And God heard their cry. Listening is the first act of his love, the first response to their suffering.

If the passion of God begins in hearing, so should ours. Listening, very often, is the first step of love. 'We should listen with the ears of God,' Dietrich Bonhoeffer has written, 'that we may speak the Word of God ... Christians, especially ministers, so often think they must always contribute something when they are in the company of others, that this is the one service they have to render. They forget that listening can be a greater service than speaking.'[8]

Listening is the primary tool with which to inform and shape our response to the needs of those around us. It is the painter's brush and the sculptor's knife. Even in silence, the world around us speaks out its need. The film *Contact*, starring Jodie Foster, tells the story of a small and dedicated scientific team who are listeners. Working shifts on a round-the-clock rota and manning a cockpit-like array of dials and gizmos, the team tune-in to signals from the furthest back corner of deep space, and listen for life. Every significant pattern in the prevailing storm of noise is amplified and analysed, as an array of dozens of huge satellite dishes comb the universe in search of intelligence. The listening team understands that listening is what they do – in fact all they do – and is a crucial element in the ongoing fight to better understand space and its workings. They are committed to listening, because listening is what it will take.

How often do you rush into speaking or action without truly listening?

> If we really want to help others we would do well to listen with all our faculties to the messages sounding out from the world around us. They can be heard through our physical environment, the media, conversations and life encounters with others, and as we listen to the turmoil that can be within our own spirits.
>
> Fran Beckett[9]

Listening skills equip us to know and understand more clearly the needs of the oppressed of our world, and by implication to hear God's heartbeat. 'We long for intimacy with God' David Westlake writes, 'and the Bible shows us

three ways of discovering it. First, we can get closer to him through our praise and worship, our prayer and relationship with him. The second is by obeying him – as he said, "Those who love me will obey my commands." The third way is this: finding him in the eyes and lives of the poor.'[10] Stop. Listen. What do you hear?

> O Lord, open my eyes that I may see the need of others, open my ears that I may hear their cries, open my heart so that they need not be without succour ... so open my eyes and my ears that I may this coming day be able to do some work of peace for thee.
>
> Alan Paton[11]

3 Mission is moving

Finally, the revelation of Yahweh at the burning bush asserts that any division between passion and action – between feelings and their expression – is false. The passions God feels flow seamlessly into the actions he takes. Feelings shape action and actions express feeling: not as two blades of a pair of scissors, nor as two sides of the same coin but inseparably, as two states of the same substance. The grammatical structure that is used in the Old Testament to speak of God *remembering* carries this sense of thought and action intertwined. In Genesis 8:1 we are told that God 'remembered' Noah and his family shut away in the ark – and in his remembering 'he sent a wind over the earth, and the waters receded.' In 1 Samuel 1:19 God 'remembers' the childless Hannah, and as a result 'in the course of time Hannah conceived and gave birth to a son.' The original text makes no distinction between the act of remembering and the actions resulting from it – they are the love of God in its liquid and its solid forms. So it is that when God remembered his promises to the Hebrew slaves, his actions on their behalf were already formulated and launched. God heard the cry of the people before he had spoken to or heard from Moses. The shepherd was drawn into the plan because God had already determined to act. Connecting with the passion of God is not simply about feeling what he feels. It begins there, but as soon as it is felt, it is already moving towards action.

Michael Landy is a passionate and committed artist who expressed his feelings in an unusual and controversial way. In a 2002 installation called *Breakdown*, he made an inventory of every item he possessed, from his Saab car to his pine bed, from the tea bags in his cupboard to the pens in his pocket. He discovered that he owned 7,220 items altogether. Over a period of two weeks these were gathered and, one by one, put through a garbage crusher installed in the former C & A store at Marble Arch, London. Credit cards went, as did treasured letters, personal jewellery, photographs and mementoes. The five tonnes of the artist's possessions, reduced to scrap, were dumped on a landfill site in Essex. Landy's actions were an expression of his art, and in an extreme form at that. But they point towards an openness to change and a willingness to let passion flow directly into actions that are haunting and memorable. God may not be calling you to feed your possessions into a garbage crusher, but what is he is asking you to do? What steps are the seamless and inevitable expressions of the passions you have begun to sense in the heart of God? Where are the feelings you have begun to feel leading you?

No one can answer these questions for you. It is here that the quest to connect with God's mission becomes personal, and responds only to your genetic imprint. But it is possible to say, for you as for me, that an encounter with the passion of God *will have* implications in action. Emotion without enaction simply does not exist in God's economy. Listen for the sound of God's heart – but look also for the imprint of his footsteps: and follow where they lead.

> We are not walking with the ghosts of the dead, we are alive with the spirit of our passion.
>
> Jamie Catto, Duncan Bridgeman and Michael Franti

WHAT IS YOUR PASSION? PART 2

if you could deal with any one single issue in your community, what would it be?

PASSION applied

Use these six questions to explore the place of passion in your own life. Where are you in the passion of God, and where is the passion of God in you?

● To what extent would you say that you 'feel what God feels' about the world? Are you someone who often talks in very passionate terms, or who takes time to see things passionately? Is this a question of temperament, or of choice?

● What are your passions? What are the subjects and ideas that produce fire in the deepest part of you – the things you would be willing to die for? Are these connected to the sense of God in your life, or kept separate in some other part of you? Should this change? Can it?

● Have your passions ever led you into trouble, when you have expressed them clumsily or impetuously? Do you have passions you see as irredeemable, or can God channel and use them in his purposes?

● Does the image of fire attract or repel you? Do you see passion as destructive, or life-giving? Which is more important for you – to find more room in your life for life-giving passion, or to give less room in your life over to destructive passion?

● How good a listener are you? Are there people and groups you simply haven't heard? When you come across people in need, are you someone who hears their cry and responds, or do you have to be prompted? Should this change? Can it?

● Where do you see God's footsteps leading? Do you have passions that you believe have a part to play in God's ultimate purpose for your life? How do you see this working out? What can you do now to nurture and express those passions?

References

1 Cited in Leonard Sweet, *Carpe Manana* (Zondervan, 2001)

2 Philip Greenslade and Selwyn Hughes, *Cover to Cover: God's Story* (Farnham: CWR, 2001) p126,128

3 Philip Greenslade and Selwyn Hughes, *Cover to Cover: God's Story* p126

4 Walter Brueggemann, *Biblical Perspectives on Evangelism*, (Abingdon Press: 1993), p55

5 Os Guinness, *The Call* (Carlisle: Spring Harvest/Authentic, 2001) p79

6 Mike Riddell, 'Fire in the Dark' Parallel Universe June 1996

7 Douglas Coupland, *Life After God* (Scribner, 2002) p175 and 178

8 Dietrich Bonhoeffer, *Life Together* (SCM, 1954)

9 Fran Beckett, *Called To Action* (Zondervan, 1989), p19

10 David Westlake, *Upwardly Mobile* (Hodder and Stoughton, 2000), p3

11 Richard J. Foster and Emilie Griffin, *Spiritual Classics: reading with the heart* (Fount, 1999), p219

■ PASSION – I will seek a connection between the deepest passions of my heart and the passion in the heart of God.

■ **PLACE – I will seek to connect with God *in* the place in which I stand, *for* the place to which he is calling me.**

■ PURPOSE – I will look for the connection between the evident purposes of my own life and the purposes of God for my context and culture.

■ POWER – I will seek to connect my strengths and my weaknesses to the power of God, and seek his transformation in both.

■ PROCESS – I will connect with the process and pace by which God has worked, is working and will work in my life.

■ PERSPECTIVE – I will look for the connection between my role in the mission of God and the wider perspective of history, finding my place in God's promise-plan.

PLACE

Habit #2 – I will seek to connect with God *in* the place in which I stand, *for* the place to which he is calling me

When you can put your church on the back of a camel, then I will believe Christianity is for us Somali camel herder

Human beings have two countries, two homelands. One is our own country, that place where each of us was born and grew up But the other is the hidden homeland of the spirit which the eye may not see and the ear may not hear but where, by our nature, we belong. Father Alexander Men

EX. 3:4 When the LORD saw that he had gone over to look, God called to him from within the bush, 'Moses! Moses!'

And Moses said, 'Here I am.'

5'Do not come any closer,' God said. 'Take off your sandals, for the place where you are standing is holy ground.' 6Then he said, 'I am the God of your father, the God of Abraham, the God of Isaac and the God of Jacob.' At this, Moses hid his face, because he was afraid to look at God. 7The LORD said, 'I have indeed seen the misery of my people in Egypt. I have heard them crying out because of their slave drivers, and I am concerned about their suffering. 8So I have come down to rescue them from the hand of the Egyptians and to bring them up out of that land into a good and spacious land,

a land flowing with milk and honey – the home of the Canaanites, Hittites, Amorites, Perizzites, Hivites and Jebusites. 9And now the cry of the Israelites has reached me, and I have seen the way the Egyptians are oppressing them. 10So now, go. I am sending you to Pharaoh to bring my people the Israelites out of Egypt.'

The bare necessities...

When I was a young teenager I was, for a time, a kind of 'apprentice hippie'. A wave of post-sixties drug culture had swept into my home city of Bath and, since many of my friends were much older, I grabbed onto the hem of their loon pants and joined in. On weekdays I was a fairly average uniformed schoolboy – apart from the twenty-six silver bangles I wore under my blazer sleeve and the faint odour of patchouli oil that followed wherever I went – but on weekends and in the holidays, I was free to join the children of the revolution. More often than not, this meant walking barefoot. The word 'shoes' was considered a swearword in our small alternative community, and as often as circumstances and the weather would allow, I went without them.

Through this lifestyle experiment I learned a lesson that is with me still: when you take off your shoes, something changes. There is a 'connection' with the ground on which you stand that is stronger and more compelling in bare feet than in shoes. Just as drivers find a freshness in their environment on the rare occasions on which they choose to leave the car behind and walk, so those used to shoes find both perspective and perceptions altered by their removal.

I think often of this when I read of Moses' encounter with Yahweh, the God of his fathers. God appears from the heart of a bush that is burning but not burned, and calls out to Moses 'Take off your sandals, for the place where you are standing is holy ground.' These words introduce a

---

HOLY GROUND

Take off your shoes and stand barefoot outside your house. What do you feel as you connect with the Place?

---

life-changing encounter that will ultimately send Moses back to Egypt for the most dramatic and reckless adventure of his eighty years. But before he can respond to the call he must receive it. Before he walks towards God's promise, he must stand in God's presence. If the first 'pin' of Moses' connection with the mission of God is passion – the connection between the deepest passions of his own heart and the passion in the heart of God – then the second is *place*. Moses encounters God *in* the midst of his ordinary life – in the place in which he stands. But the call he receives points to a place far beyond this – the place of God's promise.

The second habit of highly connected people is the habit of place – 'I will seek to connect with God *in* the place in which I stand, *for* the place to which God is calling me.'

Biblical commentators are largely agreed that God instructs Moses to take off his shoes as a means of introducing the concept of *holiness* to the encounter. This is the first time in the Bible that 'holy' is used in its noun form – the verb form appears in Genesis 2:3 referring to the seventh day of creation. The removal of shoes is a mark of respect – it sets the encounter apart as special. Moses steps trembling and vulnerable into the inner circle of God's presence, and the ordinary mountain becomes a sacred moment. But there is more here. The ground that God declares 'holy' is the very ground on which Moses stands – the mountainous

---

PHOTO MESSAGING

If you have access to a digital camera, use it to take a series of pictures of the environment in which you live. Capture shots of the people and places that make up the daily wallpaper of your life; your town; your workplace; your street; your neighbourhood. Download these images onto your computer as a slide-show, and pray as you watch it. What is God saying to you in these images? What is there that you had missed before?

---

terrain that he feels pressing against the soles of his bare feet. Before Moses can 'connect' with the distant place to which God is calling him, a place as far from his present experience as the furthest horizon Midian has to offer, he must 'connect' with God's holiness and presence right where he stands.

Imagine yourself standing in a place familiar to you – on a car park, at the football pitch, on the beach or even on your living-room carpet. Now take off your shoes. How does it change your perception of the ground on which you stand?

There are several important lessons here for contemporary disciples seeking to connect with the mission of God.

Right here, right now!

– Firstly, though the place *to* which God calls you might be anywhere – the place *in* which he calls you is always the same: it is the place in which you stand.

When the call came for Moses he was not in the place of worship but of work. He was walking the mundane paths of an insignificant life. Yet it was here that God spoke to him: this was the ground declared holy.

Many Christians struggle to know the will of God because they are haunted by two debilitating phrases – 'over there' and 'if only'. 'Over there' Christians believe the impossible – that once they get to the place of God's calling, they will hear his call. Their lives are dominated by the desperate need to be somewhere other than where they are. This may be another country, another church, another town or another job. The last thing they believe is that God will meet them where they are – but that is where he is. 'If only' Christians apply the same thinking to their circumstances. 'If only' they were richer, or poorer; or had a different set of skills or someone else's gifts; or were married, or weren't married; or had no children or had more children... then they would surely hear God's voice. 'Over there' Christians live with the assumption that a geographical shift is necessary if they are to hear the voice of God clearly. 'If only' Christians feel the same, but are looking for a circumstantial change. Both assume that it is all but impossible for God to reach them where they are. Both are wrong.

If Moses' experience is anything to go by, neither 'over there' nor 'if only' will help us. God's call may take you *to* a location a thousand miles from where you are now. He may call you *to* a place – literally or figuratively – you have never been to before. But he will call you *in* the place at which you now stand. This comes both as a reassurance and as a challenge – much as it would have done to Moses. It is reassuring because we need not fear that location or circumstances can conspire to keep God's call from reaching us. But it is also challenging because we cannot claim that we are somehow immune to God's call. There is no safe zone where the call will not get through to us. God's signal is not lost when you pass through a tunnel. If we are open, and will listen, God will speak to us: no matter how glamorous or unglamorous; how mundane or complicated are the circumstances of our lives.

Open your cage. Escape the zoo.

Futurologists often assert that 'the most reliable way to anticipate the future is by understanding the present.' Too often Christian 'calling' is seen in the future tense – it is something God will do for us at some indeterminate future time. In reality, the quality of our future encounters with God can largely be predicted from present effort. If we are not seeking him *now*, what is there to suggest that we will find him *then*? The shortest measurable distance in the known universe is the distance between where you are right now and where you need to be to hear God's voice. The only way you can silence God's call is by your own choice not to hear it.

Holy failures

– Secondly, it is those who believe themselves disqualified from serving God who most need to hear the words 'the place where you are standing is holy ground'.

Moses had any number of reasons to feel that God could not speak to him on the ground on which he stood. Midian was the place of his exile and humiliation, of his confusion and fear. He had arrived as a fugitive, fleeing the palaces and power-games of his youth. He had taken the only job open to him, as a shepherd – a role despised by Egyptian high culture; the equivalent of the Prodigal Son's much later career as a pig farmer. Everything in his immediate environment, including the bush serving time as God's temporary footstool, spoke not of destiny and of glory, but of failure, weakness, inadequacy and frustration. Midian was not a mountaintop in Moses' life; it was the deepest valley he had ever walked.

Contemporary Christians, too, have a vast range of reasons for feeling excluded from the mission of God. They are too young or too old; too spiritual or too worldly; too clever or not clever enough. To each God says 'Holy Ground'. If I say I can't serve God because I am in a second marriage or in no marriage at all since the first went down in flames – God says to me 'Holy Ground'. If I have a past my Christian friends haven't even begun to know about, God says 'Holy Ground'. When my weaknesses count me out, God says 'Holy Ground' and counts me in. The fact that Moses thought he was disqualified from serving God was the very thing that most qualified him – he knew his need. The ground on which God meets with us *is* the ground of our failure and frustration. It is made holy not by our presence but by his.

Consider the ground on which you stand – in all its ugliness. Gather together your failures and frailties, your disqualifications and doubts. Draw a circle around them all, and hear the voice of God say 'Holy Ground'.

The call of God comes as much to the weak as to the strong, as much to the failed as to the triumphant. Popular culture tells us that 'no-one remembers who came second', but it's not true. Try telling Gareth Gates, Liberty X and Sinead Quinn that there can only be one winner. The Mission of God is not an Olympic race in which the early finishers receive medals while the rest of us look on and applaud: it is a community dance; a creative weaving together of destinies in which there is a part for each of us, no matter how late we join the party. This is

> ## WE COULD BE HEROES
>
> Bring to mind people you know whom you greatly admire. Use a picture if you have one to reflect on their lives. What is it about them that inspires you? What steps have they taken in their lives to be where they are now? Could you trace – and follow – their footsteps?

the message of Jesus' parable of the workers in the vineyard. Those chosen at the first hour and those drafted in at the eleventh hour were equally and generously rewarded. God's upside-down kingdom does not operate according to standard rules. It has an inner logic of its own: the logic by which the last will be first and the first last; by which a few grains of yeast change the very nature of a batch of dough; by which the mustard seed defies all expectations to become a semi-detached mansion for the birds. Moses had written 'disqualified' across his own life, but God tore up the label. The classic directions mumbled by the old Cornish farmer, 'You can't get there from here' are precisely the reverse of God's ways. Whatever God will call you to, the truth is that you *can* get there from here: and you can start the journey now.

Hide and speak

– Thirdly, while God's call may be extraordinary, it is mediated to us through the fabric and furniture of our ordinary lives.

Theologian Karl Rahner wrote, 'I now see clearly that, if there is any path at all on which I can approach You, it must lead through the very middle of my ordinary daily life. If I should try to flee to You by any other way, I'd actually be leaving myself behind, and that, aside from being quite impossible, would accomplish nothing at all.'[1]

The F-117A fighter plane was developed by the US Air Force to be invisible to radar. The stealth technology employed was so successful that the floor of the hangar in which the planes were housed would often be littered with the battered bodies of dead bats: their built-in echolocation system having totally failed to 'notice' the huge planes.

One of the things we learn by experience is that God hides from us in order to be found. Like a child playing hide-and-seek, his disguises are not intended to keep us from seeing him, but to give us the joy of finding him. He hides in the ordinary things of our lives in order to jump out and surprise us – a sure-fire way to get our attention when he wants to speak to us. For Moses, God hid behind a bush when he knew the shepherd would pass nearby. He did this, the narrative tells us, to catch Moses' eye. If Moses had been blind to the surprises hidden in the world around him; if he had no interest beyond caring for his sheep; if he had been entirely fixed on getting from point A to point B across the mountainside with neither diversion nor distraction – he would have ignored

the bush and missed the discovery of God. How often do we look at the world around us and not see God through his disguises? How often do we pass him in the street and not notice? If he whispers our name, do we hear him? God's favourite game is hide-and-speak – are we too busy and important to play?

> **Ever been to Croydon* and seen God? (*Substitute Colchester, Moscow, Oklahoma or other as necessary)**

One of the actors involved in the children's show *The Tweenies* had a young son of his own who had learning difficulties. Every day when Dad went off to work, he would kiss his son goodbye before heading off to dress as the character 'Mylo' and pretend to be in pre-school all day. His son, meanwhile, would get home from his own school as early as possible so as not to miss his favourite TV programme – *The Tweenies*. He loved the show and watched every episode, and he had a favourite character: Mylo. As soon as his father came home from work, he would run to throw his arms round him. His dad would ask how his day had been and if he'd enjoyed *The Tweenies*. The boy's eyes would light up: he thought it was the best show on earth and Mylo was just the greatest. They would talk together for a few moments about the antics of Mylo – the son revelling in the joy *The Tweenies* had brought him and the father warmed by the reflection of that same joy. But here's the secret – this boy didn't know what his dad did for a job. He had

---

HIDE AND SPEAK

If God was looking in your life for the equivalent of a bush to hide in, what would he set fire to? Has he?

---

no idea that when he sat in front of the TV to watch Mylo, he was watching his own father at work.

> Today we, the children of Western culture, post-modern, adult children of the enlightenment, struggle with practical atheism. Our churches are slowly emptying and, more and more, the sense of God is slipping from our ordinary lives. ... The road back to a lively faith is not a question of finding the right answers, but of living a certain way, contemplatively. The existence of God, like the air we breathe, need not be proven. It is more a question of developing good lungs to meet it correctly. ... We must live in such a way as to give birth to God in our lives.
>
> Ronald Rolheiser[2]

Vocation on location

The path to finding more of the presence of God in our lives does not lie in seeking more and more extraordinary events and experiences – it lies in better under-standing and interpreting the events and experiences around us. God is there to be found, a hidden presence woven into the fabric of our ordinary lives. The question is whether we will see and hear the God who is trying to catch our attention. An instant after he had caught sight of the bush that was burning yet unburned, Moses made a choice to take a closer look. He didn't have to stop, but he didn't hear the voice of God until he had done so. The most important decision he ever made was the decision, in the midst of the ordinary, to explore the extraordinary presence of God.

Jean-Pierre de Caussade was a spiritual director in seventeenth-century France. He developed a day-by-day spirituality built on the foundation of the 'sacrament of the present moment'. This was the view that the here and now is sacred, no matter how I have arrived at it, because it is in the here and now that God will speak to me. If it is true that God, in his providence, has allowed me to come to the place in which I stand, with all the trials and tasks that shape me, then it must also be true that he can speak to me here. The present moment is sacred because it is the only moment I have to respond to God's love. The ground on which I stand is holy because it is the only ground from which I can produce a 'yes' to God. 'To discover God in the smallest and most ordinary things, as well as in the greatest,' de Caussade wrote, 'is to possess a rare and sublime faith ... A living faith is nothing else than a steadfast pursuit of God through all that disguises, disfigures, demolishes and seeks, so to speak, to abolish him ... Nothing is hidden from his eyes. He walks alike over the smallest blade of grass, the tallest cedars, grains of sand or rocky mountains. Wherever you go he has gone before. Only follow him and you will find him everywhere.'[3]

The spark glows on...

I love this poem, which I think of as a 'poem of place'. It was written by Annie Brierley, who was working at the time in a centre for the mentally ill. Annie wanted to capture the sense that even in this place of despair, there was hope – and she did so, I believe, beautifully. The poem is called The Patient.

He sits.
Those around him flirt, shout, weep, turn up the radio.
Someone tries to put their fist through the window.
He sits.

Nurse's voices mingle with those in the patients' minds.
Silent smiles amongst the staff.
A special smile for him.
No response.

In front of him is an NHS coffee table,
Half a pack of cigarettes,

And a slagheap of discarded butts
In a lurid ashtray
An ex-patient has made.
Like a smoking machine
He lights up; puffs furiously;
Puts it out; half-smoked.
And again. And again.

Why does he chain-smoke but never finish them?
Part of his other world,
Or a half-remembered health warning?
No-one knows – he doesn't talk.
(Few people can tell, but this is a good day).

He reaches to stub out another one, but it won't.
Gently it smoulders in a pile of waste.
Semi-frenetic, he pokes at it.
Defiantly it glows.

A nurse passes: smiles a delighted smile
At the discovered animation.
A smile back.

In a pile of ashes,
The spark glows on.[4]

PEOPLE-MAPS

Draw a 'people-map' of your life as a series of concentric circles. Start with your 'inner circle' – people and commitments at the very heart of your life. Add to this the people or commitments you interact with on a daily basis, then those you interact with regularly but less frequently. Add those you rarely see, but are linked to, then those in your environment you are aware of but not involved in. You will tend to use names in the inner circles, but categories further out, such as 'colleagues at work', 'those who live in the same close', 'those I see at the bus stop' etc. You can also name those who are distant from you, but connected.

Now take some time to reflect on the evident needs of these people. Where do you sense the passion of God stirring, or your own compassion being aroused? Use red crayons to mark the 'hot spots' of need. Where are the forgotten people – those whose cries you haven't heard? Mark these 'cold spots' with green crayon. Reflect on the 'hot spots' and the 'cold spots' on your people-map, and on your response to them.

Sacred spaces

Our failure to hear the whisper of God in our world stems, very often, from our impoverished expectations. We have never been taught to expect the voice of God in an ordinary bush – and as a result we miss it when it comes. Margaret Silf suggests that the presence of God is a mystery woven into the very fabric of the world in which we live – but that all too often we fail to perceive it.

> The mystery of all we are seeking may take the form of the everyday, and we may fail to recognise it, precisely because it is so 'normal', just as Mary failed at first to recognise 'the gardener'. If we really desire to reach the meaning beyond the veil, we may need to become much more sensitively aware of the immediacy and the mystery of the created world around us.[5]

The end result of an encounter with God *in* the place in which you stand is that you become less frantic and more trusting about the place *to* which he is calling you. Rather than being a place that you are desperate to get to in the shortest possible time, your calling becomes a place to which God is leading you in his time. You are no longer looking for everything to fall into place in an instant, nor are you frustrated each day by your lack of progress. Rather, you are walking with God on a path he has chosen for you, towards a destiny that he himself has guaranteed. Christian security is not about how soon you arrive – it is about who you travel with.

Is God speaking to you through the here and now of your situation and location? Are the words that carry his call hidden in the needs of those around you, in the unexpected shafts of grace that fall like sunlight across a dusty room? Is he trying to get your attention, to slow you down and take the shoes from your feet? Is God a hitch-hiker on the verge of your life, while you pass by without thinking because you're driving too fast to stop? 'The surprises of life come in many different guises,' writes Margaret Silf. 'How easy to miss them completely, especially if we have preconceived ideas about how they are supposed to happen.'[6]

Stop. Listen. Who do you hear?

Far horizons

The result of Moses' encounter with God *in* the place in which he stood was that he was called to look towards a far-distant horizon. God introduced him to the possibility of change, and the promise of a place of freedom for the nation of Israel. Moses heard the call wearing the humble robe and bare feet of a shepherd, but the words he heard spoke of something much greater. If the context of the call is remarkable for its ordinariness, the content is anything but. Israel have won the Lottery, received a big tax refund and been selected to appear on *Blind Date*, all on the same day. God has not set out simply to answer their prayer for relief from the cruel bondage of Egypt – he is going to give them the desires of their hearts.

Definition: MEOPIA – vocational short-sightedness. The failure or refusal to see God on the horizon, for fear of losing sight of me in the middle distance.

Moses is introduced to a paradox that marks the lives of those called by God. He is told at one and the same time to look down and to look up. Looking down, he connects with the ground on which he stands and meets God there. His relationship with Yahweh is not based on a fantasy or deception – it is earthed in the harsh realities of failure and compromise. But he must also look up – to a place so far from his current experience that he can barely make it out, shimmering on the horizon. Moses is asked to believe that God will lead his people to a land 'flowing with milk and honey' – a land of prosperity and peace. The freeing of the slaves is not the final goal towards which God is working, but merely a step along the way. What God has in store for Israel outweighs ten-fold the highest expectations Moses would have dared to entertain.

Imagine the best thing that could happen in the place for which you are concerned. Picture the best possible outcome – the result that would leave you reeling with joy, in no doubt of the reality of God's favour. Now ask God, 'Is this the outcome I should pray for?' The place *to* which God was calling Moses was as far beyond his earlier expectations as a space flight is beyond cycling. To even begin to see what God was promising, he had to lift

---

FAR HORIZONS

Reflect on the people, places, situations or spheres of activity that have been 'far horizons' in your life. These will be areas that often fill your thoughts, or that stir your passion whenever you come across them. Examples I have known include individuals who are fascinated by South American peoples and cultures, or who feel compassion stirring whenever they encounter or remember people fighting addictions. Others are moved by the needs of children, or inexplicably drawn to everything French. Whatever the 'far horizons' of your life are, ask yourself

- Is this the beginning of God's call on my life?

- What can I do to find out more?

- How can I nurture this in prayer and test it in relationship?

---

his eyes; to increase his expectations; to raise his hopes.

> If God can do more than you can imagine, why not ask for more imagination?
>
> Dan Davidson

Moses removed his sandals because he knew, or sensed at least, that *here* and *now* were important words in God's vocabulary. He wasn't going to run away, nor would he pass by on the other side of God's strange interruption of his day. He was ready to stop, listen and learn. Rooted to the spot on the ground of the everyday, he heard a fresh word of promise and hope: a new beginning smuggled unexpectedly into the life of an old man. In the sacredness of the present moment, on the holy ground of his failure and frustration, Moses heard the voice of God, and was changed. Because he was able to connect with God *in* the place in which he stood, he received a call *for* the place God had reserved for him: and entered into his unique place in God's purposes.

What would have to change in your life if you were to develop the habit of hearing God *in* the place in which you stand *for* the place to which he's calling you?

O Lord God, Creator of all.
Open my eyes to beauty
Open my mind to wonder
Open my ears to others
Open my heart to you.

David Adam[7]

PLACE applied

Use these six questions to explore the dynamic of 'place' in your own life. Where do you see God in relation to the place you now stand and the place to which he may be calling you?

● When was the last time you walked barefoot? How did it feel? Did it give you a greater connection with the ground over which you walked? What do you think it might mean to 'take off your shoes' in terms of the place you now stand spiritually?

● Where do you stand? What defines your life right now – work? family? sickness? Think about the things that mark out the ground on which you stand. Can God speak to you here? Can it be holy ground?

● Is the idea that God can speak to you right where you are strange to you, or perfectly acceptable? If you don't believe God can speak to you 'here and now', explore why not – is it because of who God is or isn't, or because of who you are? Should this change? Can it?

● What are your weaknesses? What have you failed at? Where do you feel inadequate? Have you heard God say anything to you through these experiences?

● Has God ever surprised you by turning up in your daily life? If he wanted to jump out on you, where would he hide? Are there places in your life in which you NEVER sense the presence of God? Look more closely – where might he be hiding?

● What are your 'far horizons'? Has God spoken into your life about his plans and promises for your future? Do you have a clear view of this, or just hints? Are there ways in which you can bring into focus the picture of the future God is showing you?

References

1 Tony Lane, *Concise History of Christian Thought* (Oxford: Lion)

2 Ronald Rolheiser, *The Shattered Lantern: rediscovering the felt presence of God* (London: Hodder and Stoughton, 1994)

3 Jean-Pierre de Caussade, *The Sacrament of the Present Moment* (Zondervan, 1996)

4 Annie Brierley, unpublished material created at a Spring Harvest poetry workshop, 1999

5 Margaret Silf, *Sacred Spaces – Stations on a Celtic Way* (Lion, 2002)

6 Margaret Silf, *Sacred Spaces – Stations on a Celtic Way* (Lion, 2002)

7 David Adam, *Power Lines*, (Triangle, 1992)

- **PASSION** – I will seek a connection between the deepest passions of my heart and the passion in the heart of God.

- **PLACE** – I will seek to connect with God *in* the place in which I stand, *for* the place to which he is calling me.

- **PURPOSE** – I will look for the connection between the evident purposes of my own life and the purposes of God for my context and culture.

- **POWER** – I will seek to connect my strengths and my weaknesses to the power of God, and seek his transformation in both.

- **PROCESS** – I will connect with the process and pace by which God has worked, is working and will work in my life.

- **PERSPECTIVE** – I will look for the connection between my role in the mission of God and the wider perspective of history, finding my place in God's promise-plan.

PURPOSE

Habit #3 – I will look for the connection between the evident purposes of my own life and the purposes of God for my context and culture

> " Where Jesus is, there is life, the synoptic Gospels tell us. There sick life is healed, saddened life is given fresh heart, marginalised life is accepted, captive life is freed, and the tormenting spirits of death are driven out... The mission of Jesus and the mission of the Spirit are nothing other than movements of life: movements of healing, of liberation, of righteousness and justice. Jesus didn't bring a new religion into the world. What he brought was new life.
> Jurgen Moltmann[1]
>
> **You are not how much you have in the bank. You are not the contents of your wallet. You are not your job.** *Fight Club* "

EX. 3:7 *The LORD said, 'I have indeed seen the misery of my people in Egypt. I have heard them crying out because of their slave drivers, and I am concerned about their suffering. So I have come down to rescue them from the hand of the Egyptians and to bring them up out of that land into a good and spacious land, a land flowing with milk and honey – the home of the Canaanites, Hittites, Amorites, Perizzites, Hivites and Jebusites. And now the cry of the Israelites has reached me, and I have seen the way the Egyptians are oppressing them. So now, go. I am sending you to Pharaoh to bring my people the Israelites out of Egypt.'*

What's in the box?

The world is full of useful objects we rarely get the chance to use, but need desperately at certain key moments. The presentation box that an engagement ring comes in, is one. For most of our lives before and after the proposal it is barely relevant. Unless you keep it until your children lose their first teeth and want to keep them safe, it will rarely find another purpose. But in the proposal itself – from the nervous preparation and approach when it is endlessly fumbled and fiddled with in the jacket pocket to the moment of truth when for a brief instant it is centre-

---

DESIGNED FOR LIFE

Think of the engagement box and the warning triangle: objects made for a purpose. On the basis of your design and make up, do you have some idea of what you were made for? If you asked the question 'Why did God create me?', would you have an answer?

---

stage in floodlit glory – the box is the focus of history and changes lives. The ring-box's purpose is limited and specific, but when it serves that purpose it is glorious.

Another boxed object that I have carried in the boot of my car for many years but rarely had occasion to use is the warning triangle. This ingenious device spends most of its life folded into a red plastic box, but every now and then, in moments of great need, it is taken out. Its glaring fluorescent plumage is unfurled and it stands guard, proud as a peacock, on the verge of a busy road. It warns approaching motorists and very possibly saves lives. As a triangle it has few, if any, other uses. If you turned up with it to the rehearsals of the London Symphony Orchestra and asked to join as triangle player, you would not be well received. If you took it to your local pool hall and tried to set up the tables, you would cause confusion and disarray. Applied in the wrong setting, it is useless. Applied in the right setting, it can save lives. Why? Because the warning triangle is an object with a purpose. Like the ring-box, it has been made for a specific task, and only comes into its own when focused on that

task. It is at its best when fulfilling the purpose for which it was designed.

The Shepherd's Bush triangle

The image of a 'triangle with a purpose' is vital to the understanding of Moses' call. The narrative establishes God's purposes by triangulation from three different points. These are the three forces active in the call of Moses, and it is in the dynamic tension established among the three that the old shepherd found his purpose and direction. The Exodus narrative is the unfolding story of the love triangle amongst Yahweh, Moses and the Hebrew slaves.

We have already seen that the passion in the heart of God for his people was foundational to this story, and that it met, resonated with and redirected the passions of Moses' own heart. But it took a third factor to transform this passion into purpose, and this was the 'outward focus' of the plight of the slaves. The story could not be told if it involved only God and Moses. Thrilling as that narrative might be, it would not be the great adventure we have before us. In every encounter between Moses and God, in every prayer and conversation, there is this third party – sometimes physically present, sometimes absent but always remembered. The passion shared between Yahweh and Moses has a purpose – it is a directed passion. It does not float unconnectedly between them, but flows towards a shared goal: the liberation of the people God has chosen.

Moses discovers that God has an inner compass, pulled inexorably towards the magnetic north of his people's need, and that he, too, is drawn by this same goal. He has been confused by this force in the past and has never known what to do with it, but it has been the defining force of his adult life. This is why he couldn't enjoy the long-term benefits of royal adoption. This is why he couldn't 'let things lie'. This is the root and source of his exile and dislocation. It is when he sees that the flow of his own heart and life and the arrows of the passion of God are pointing to the same goal that he steps into purpose.

Purposeful living is defined by the triangle of three forces:

– The passion, plans and purposes of God

– The gifts, instincts, urges and longings of my own heart

– The evident need of the human family

Religion assumes that you can be consumed by the first in isolation.

Humanism assumes that the second is enough. Secularism lives predominantly in the third. Effective mission insists that all three voices must be heard. This is the triangle of purpose – the zone in which it is possible to identify and engage with the purposes of God, to find personal growth and fulfilment and to love and serve your fellow human beings: and not to allow any one of the three to be withered or distorted by lack of attention to another. Jesus was sketching out the boundaries of this zone when he was asked to sum up God's Law.

> 'Love the Lord your God with all your heart and with all your soul and with all your mind.' This is the first and greatest commandment. And the second is like it: 'Love your neighbour as yourself.' All the Law and the Prophets hang on these two commandments (Mt. 22:37).

You, God, your neighbour – the perfect love triangle

The triangle of purpose that is present in the Shepherd's Bush encounter becomes the template for the remainder of Moses' life. The book of Exodus is an interweaving of three different biographies – it is the story of Yahweh, it is the story of Moses and it is the story of the people of Israel. Throughout the narrative, it is the interplay between these three that provides the drama.

Whatever purpose God has prepared for your life, you can be sure that it will draw you into this triangle. God's purpose for you will serve three goals at once:

- It will bring fulfilment to the passion and potential that God has invested in your personality – the call of God gives ultimate expression to your identity. Calling throws light on *who you are*.

- It will move towards the liberation and salvation of humanity – meeting the needs of those on whom the love of God is focused. Calling releases human beings *to be who they were created to be*.

- It will contribute to the fulfilment of God's purposes for the whole earth – the call of God is born in the character of God. Calling is an expression of *who God is*.

Understanding, exploring, enjoying and fulfilling the call of God implied, for Moses, stepping into this three-way adventure. He was called, in effect, to know God, to know himself and to know the needs of the people. Clues to finding the purpose of God for your life can be gleaned from all three of these dimensions, and a sure sign that you are on the right track is that a balance is established among the three: when you discover that the things you are doing fit into God's plan, make sense of who you are and meet the needs of others. As Moses stepped into God's purposes, he discovered that he was stepping into his true identity, moving on in the love and service of others and engaging with God's plans for the world.

Step into identity

Come take a ride

The film *Men in Black* told the unorthodox tale of Agents J and K, Will Smith and Tommy Lee Jones respectively. Star members of the highly secretive agency of the film's title, the pair were tasked with monitoring and controlling the presence of alien 'guests' on earth, and in particular with dealing with the rogues – 'protecting the earth from the scum of the universe'. The sequel, *MIIB*, picks up the story after the retirement of Agent K (Jones), with Agent J (Smith) test-driving a series of new partners. A crisis arises, and it becomes necessary to bring 'K' out of retirement. The problem with this proposal is that 'K' has been 'neuralyzed' – his memory has been wiped of every trace of the Men in Black and their alien customers. He is working in blissful tranquillity in a regional sub-post office entirely unaware of the life he once lived. He has forgotten who he is.

J goes to the post office to persuade K to be de-neuralyzed, but he meets with little co-operation. Even when K's new work colleagues are all revealed to be disguised aliens, the penny does not drop. In desperation, J reaches for the part of K's memory that he knows has not been lost. 'When you look up at the stars at night,' he says, 'you get a feeling deep down in your gut that you don't know who you are – like you know more about what's going on out there than you do

THE TRIANGLE OF PURPOSE

Draw a large triangle on a piece of paper: large enough to take up most of the sheet. Label its three points as:

- The purposes and passions of God

- The purposes and passions of my own heart

- The evident needs of the world

Now think about where in the triangle you are placed. Are you clearer about God's purposes than about your part in them? Are you more aware of your own needs and aspirations than about those of others? Are you aware of the needs of others, but at the expense of your sense of self-awareness or of God's plan? Think which of the three points you are closest to, and which you are furthest from – and what it might take to establish a good balance of the three.

down here ... If you decide you want to know who you really are, you come take a ride with me ...'

> You can't think your way out of a box, you've got to act.
>
> Tom Peters

This dramatic moment is remarkably close to the conversation between Yahweh and Moses at the burning bush. The shepherd's first response to the magnitude of God's call is to ask 'Who am I?' A little later he will turn the question around and ask God 'Who are you?', but his first thoughts are of his own struggle with confidence and self-awareness. And God's answer is instructive. He does not tell Moses directly who he is, but says, rather, 'I will be with you.' It is in stepping into God's purposes that Moses will find his true identity. Believing that God has made a wise choice, he must trust the

judgement of his Maker and move forward. 'If you want to know who you really are, come take a ride with me.'

> Purpose is that deepest dimension within us – our central core or essence – where we have a profound sense of who we are, where we came from, and where we are going. God is still inviting disciples to discover the difference their lives can make if they, like Jesus, make God's purposes their purposes.
>
> Tom and Christine Sine[2]

It is in the very nature of God's 'triangle of purpose' that our identity is hidden in our destiny. The one who calls us is the one who made us. As we step into his purposes, we will find ourselves more and more aware that the shoes we are wearing are a perfect fit.

LIVING ON PURPOSE

Get hold of a copy of Tom and Christine Sine's book *Living on purpose*. Work through this, making note of the places where it touches particularly on your situation.

Rabbi Zusya ... said 'When I stand before God I will not be asked "Why were you not Moses?" but "Why were you not Zusya?"'

John Glass

It was not easy for Moses to connect with the purposes of God. There were many years of wandering and wondering, and not a few false starts. But once he stepped into the shoes God offered him, he could not doubt the fit. He was uniquely qualified for the role God had in mind – no one else with Hebrew blood could even dream of approaching Pharaoh: he wouldn't even take the call. Try calling 10 Downing Street or the White House, giving your name and asking to be put through to Blair or Bush. Unless your name is known and provable, you won't get past the first operator. Moses had access because God had so engineered his life as to make access possible, but until he connected with God's plan, bringing all of himself into the triangle, his past was of no use to him. In the triangle, every aspect of his past – the good, the bad and the ugly – found resolution.

Do you have a reason for being, a focused sense of purpose in your life? Or is your life the product of shifting resolutions and the myriad pulls of forces outside yourself? Do you want to go beyond success to significance? Have you come to realise that self-reliance always falls short and that world-denying solutions provide no answer in the end? Listen to Jesus of Nazareth; answer his call.

Os Guinness[4]

Douglas Coupland is not alone in feeling the 'dystopia' of contemporary consumer lifestyles. 'I was the biggest loser in the world,' he writes in *Life after God*, 'I couldn't even get mad. I groaned with despair, not even knowing if retracing my path would make any difference because I wasn't sure where the correct forks were.'[3] Many, many people struggle over years to come to a true and valued sense of who they are. Like undiscovered antiques, they live with themselves for decades without realising either their unique provenance or their intrinsic worth. It takes a visit from God's *Antiques Roadshow* – in Moses' case a fire in a bush – to bring the quest for identity to the surface. The key is to 'make the connection' with God's mission. Move towards your purpose in God's plan, and you will move towards your true self and identity. Connect with God's mission and you will connect with the true you.

Do you want to find out who you really are? Step into partnership with your Creator, and the rest will be history.

IDENTIKIT

There is an old child's game where you draw the head of a character and fold the paper over before adding a body, then legs, then feet. Try applying the same principle to your own identity. On a piece of paper, complete the sentence 'I am ...' Immediately fold the paper to conceal what you have written. Now add another 'I am ...' statement. Fold under again, and so on, until you have written six to ten statements. Now open out the paper and look at all your 'I ams' together. If this is who you are, where does the primary sense of God's purpose lie for you? Pray about any discoveries you make.

Move on in love and service of others

> If you are in doubt, apply the following test: recall the face of the poorest and weakest person you may have seen and ask yourself if the step you contemplate is going to be of any use to them.
>
> Mahatma Gandhi

As Moses stepped into a dynamic connection with the purposes of God, he found that his connection with those he was called to serve also grew. He had tried to connect with his blood-tribe earlier in his life, but had been rejected. Exile in Midian was for Moses not only exile from the Egyptian court but also from the slave community. His longing to help those in need could not be usefully expressed – until his calling at Shepherd's Bush. From this point on he found his strong desire to help the oppressed fulfilled beyond his

wildest expectations. Connection with God did not disconnect him from the needs of the world, but took him deeper in. This is an acid test of the authenticity of biblical spirituality. If your devotion to God makes the needs of the world seem more distant, there is a grave danger that it is escapism, not faith, you are expressing. On the other hand, if you immerse yourself in the needs of the world without looking to the other side of the triangle – connecting with God as source – you will quickly reach burn-out. It is only as the triangle is balanced that you find you have something to offer, and can bring blessing to those in need.

John Piper expresses this well in his consideration of Jesus' command to 'love your neighbour as yourself'. 'Jesus commands, "As you love yourself, so love your neighbour",' he writes

> Which means: As you long for food when you are hungry, so long to

feed your neighbour when he is hungry. As you long for nice clothes for yourself, so long for nice clothes for your neighbour. As you desire to have a comfortable place to live, so desire a comfortable place to live for your neighbour. As you seek to be safe and secure from calamity and violence, so seek comfort and security for your neighbour. As you seek friends for yourself, so be a friend to your neighbour. As you want your life to count and be significant, so desire that same significance for your neighbour. As you work to make good grades yourself, so work to help your neighbour make good grades. As you like to be welcomed into strange company, so welcome your neighbour into strange company ... In other words' make the measure of your self-seeking the measure of your self-giving. The word 'as' is very radical: 'Love your neighbour AS yourself'. It means: If you are energetic in pursuing your own happiness, be energetic in pursuing the happiness of your neighbour. If you are creative in pursuing your own happiness, be creative in pursuing the happiness of your neighbour. In other words Jesus is not just saying: seek for your neighbour the same things you seek for yourself, but seek them in the same way – the same zeal and energy and creativity and perseverance. Make the measure of your self-seeking the measure of your self-giving. Measure your pursuit of the happiness of others by the pursuit of your own. How do you pursue your own well

Table of 'Values moving toward the kingdom'

Value	Today's distorted version	More kingdom-like version
Loyalty	Only to our family	To all in our community
View of Person	Only powerful matter	All men, women and children matter
Compassion	For those who can help us	For those who are in need
Repentance	Only if caught	Personal responsibility for wrong
Forgiveness	Only to our equals	To all who injure us
Sharing	Only with our family	With all who are in need
Equality	For those who own land	For all men and women
Justice	Only for the powerful	For all, even the weakest
Peacemaking	Within the family	Within the community and world[6]

being? Pursue your neighbour's well being that way, too.[5]

Bryant L. Myers takes this message further by suggesting that the love we show to those close to us can be extended to a wider circle, as we ask the question 'Who is my neighbour?' He contrasts the contemporary distortion of neighbour love with the more holistic possibilities of a kingdom orientation. This very practical approach allows each of us to test our own responses, and to find a place to start. Have we been selfish with the blessings of God, assuming that whatever God gives us is for us alone – or do we know what it is to extend love and blessing beyond ourselves to those in need? If this outward side of the triangle of purpose in our lives is weak, what steps can we take to strengthen it?

> Millions of North Americans and Western Europeans are in despair as they seek in vain for happiness through ever greater material abundance. The idolatrous mater-ialism of the economic rat race creates alcoholics, ruined marriages and heart attacks. Jesus, on the other hand, offers true joy – not through getting, but through giving.[7]
>
> Ron Sider

The outward dimension of God's call reflects the fact that all our actions, whether intended or not, affect and impact the lives of others. Global reporter John Simpson captures this movingly in his report of a chance meeting with Mikhail Kalashnikov, inventor of the assault rifle that has taken his name to every troubled corner of the globe:

> His modesty was admirable; and yet in terms of the effects of what he had done – the number of people killed and the amount of misery caused – I have never met anyone worse in my life. He might merely have been in charge of designing the machinery; but it was the machinery, in its extraordinary efficiency, which did the damage. Andrei Sakharov, having been the father of the Soviet Union's nuclear weapons, became the country's leading political dissident. Mikhail Kalashnikov, one of the few ordinary Russians whose name is known in every country in the world, felt no remorse, and later went into politics on his own account. Perhaps it doesn't matter: his remorse would not have saved a single life. But the basic point is that you do not have to be evil to do evil. In an industrial and post-industrial world, it is sometimes enough merely to be efficient.[8]

PURPOSE BY DEFAULT

Everybody's work produces something. The Hebrew slaves built pyramids and palaces. Mikhail Kalashnikov designed a rifle. What is produced by the labours you are engaged in? Think beyond the immediate result to the longer-term implications – what legacy are you leaving the world?

> The unsettling combination of celebrated brand names and impoverished production conditions have turned Nike, Disney and Wal-mart, among others, into powerful metaphors for a brutal new way of doing business. In a single image, the brand-name sweatshop tells the story of the obscene disparities of the global economy: corporate executives and celebrities raking in salaries so high they defy comprehension, billions of dollars spent on branding and advertising – all propped up by a system of shanty-towns, squalid factories and the misery and trampled expectations of young women like the ones I met in Cavite, struggling to survive.
>
> Naomi Klein[9]

*Dearest Lord, teach me to be
  generous;*
*Teach me to serve Thee as Thou
  deservest;*
To give and not to count the cost,
To fight and not to heed the wounds,
To toil and not to seek the rest,
*To labour and not to ask for any
  reward,*
*Save that of knowing that I do Thy
  will.*

St Ignatius Loyola (1491–1556)

It is only as we acknowledge the second side of the triangle, and look for signs of the purposes of God in the impact of our lives on the world, that we can begin to make the kind of difference God looks for in us. Just as Moses sought the purposes of God in the culture and context in which he lived so must we, in a world of injustice and oppression, ask the question 'How then should we live?'

Engage with God's plans for the world

If the first surprise for Moses was the depth of God's passion for his people and the second was that he had a part to play, the third was the global scale of God's purposes. In the early chapters of Exodus it might appear that getting the slaves out of Egypt is enough. The sheer audacity of this goal is as great a target as climbing Mount Everest or sailing single-handed round the world might be today. It is hard even to think beyond this achievement – but the unfolding narrative makes clear that this is just a step in the much larger plan to which God is working.

> The best way to make your dreams come true is to wake up!
>
> Paul Valery

In Exodus 19:4, God reminds Moses: 'You yourselves have seen what I did to Egypt, and how I carried you on eagles' wings and brought you to myself. Now if you obey me fully and keep my covenant, then out of all nations you will be my treasured possession. Although the whole earth is mine, you will be for me a kingdom of priests and a holy nation.' These are the words you are to speak to the Israelites.'

Mark Stibbe explains the importance of God's choice of Israel. 'God chose Israel out of all the nations of the world to be his adopted son,' he writes, 'He chose one of the most insignificant groups of people and, in the process, made them the most significant nation in history. He took a very ordinary community of people and conferred on them the most extraordinary purpose. Why? Because our God is an adopting Father. Out of sheer grace he chooses to embrace people in the enfolding circle of his love.'[10]

As Moses steps forward in the purposes of God for his life, he finds himself active in this much larger arena. God gives him a place in a plan of cosmic proportions. His acceptance of God's call enables the people of Israel to enter, in turn, into their destiny, and God allows him to glimpse the significance of his role in this wider picture. His 'micro' response to the purposes of God is shown to connect with God's 'macro' plan.

There are 86,400 seconds in a day. What will you do today?

> The affirmation is that the Yahweh, the God who had chosen Israel, was also the creator, owner and Lord of the whole world (Deut. 10:14f), and that Yahweh had chosen Israel in relation to his purpose for the world, not just for Israel. The election of Israel was not tantamount to a rejection of the nations, but explicitly for their ultimate benefit. Thus, rather than asking if Israel itself 'had a mission', in the sense of being 'sent' anywhere, we need to see the missional nature of Israel's existence in relation to the mission of God in the world. Israel's mission was to be something, not to go somewhere.
>
> Christopher Wright[11]

> Salvation includes the healing of broken relationships – with God, with others, with nature. It includes the healing of persons, justice for the oppressed and stewardship of the natural world. It operates on many levels – spiritual, psychological, physical, economic, social and political. No aspect of the creation lies outside God's desire to bring restoration and wholeness.
>
> Clark Pinnock and Robert C. Brow[12]

Connecting with God's plan of salvation does not necessarily mean 'becoming an evangelist' – though for some it will. Nor is it only to do with 'personal witness' and the eternal future of your friends. In the biblical view, salvation is concerned with the healing of broken relationships – with God, with others, with the natural world. 'Shalom', the full-orbed, multi-dimensional peace that comes whenever the kingdom of God is established, operates on many levels – spiritual, psychological, physical, economic, social and political. Everything we see was created by God, everything we see has been touched by the fall – and everything we see is included in the promise of redemption. We begin to connect with God's mission in every arena when we wrestle with the question – what does redemption mean in this arena? How has sin deprived the world of the God-given blessings of the creation? How might the resurrection power of Jesus make the difference?

Feeding the poor; playing football; presenting evangelistic events; staging plays and art exhibitions; shopping for old people; campaigning for justice; engaging in party political affairs; creating and using wealth; skateboarding; clubbing; writing; recording... all these can and do have a legitimate place in God's purposes. Whether they look on the surface like worthy causes or leisure pursuits, they are transformed into God's mission when they are undertaken in response to his word and in obedience to the promptings of his Spirit.

This is the unique feature of a personal sense of purpose derived from connection to the mission of God. On the field of battle we see only the campaigns in which we fight – but God sees the whole war, and enables us to know that our small acts have significance on a global scale. What greater source of motivation can there be than to know, by the sheer generosity of God's grace, that your small acts of obedience are woven into his planet-wide tapestry of redemption?

Peace, shalom, the all-embracing blessing of the God of Israel – this is what the presence of the kingdom is. The church is a movement launched into the life of the world to bear in its own life God's gift of peace for the life of the world.

Lesslie Newbigin[13]

When playwright Vaclav Havel was elected as the first President of post-communist Czechoslovakia, he spoke openly of the need for personal transformation as a means of global change. 'What could change the direction of today's civilisation?' he asked.

It is my deep conviction that the only option is a change in the sphere of the spirit, in the sphere of human conscience. It's not enough to invent new machines, new regulations, new institutions. We must develop a new understanding of the true purpose of our existence on earth. Only by making such a fundamental shift will we be able to create new models of behaviour and a new set of values for the planet.

The answer to Havel's initial question can be summed up in two words – *connected people*. It is people who have found their place in the mission of God, connecting with their Maker and making his goals their goals, who find themselves part of the redemption of creation, bringing shalom to every corner of our world. History-makers are found amongst those prepared to wrestle with their own identity, with the nature of God and with his purposes for the planet.

Jacob wrestled with an angel,
Jesus argued with the Devil.
To be holy is to struggle
Free from every kind of evil.

You've got to struggle –
You've got to fight for freedom.

The Late, Late Service, Glasgow

INTERLUDE: FOLLOWING THE SPIRIT INTO MISSION

To Russia with love

A couple of years ago I first visited Saratov, a city of roughly one million people on the banks of the Volga, about an hour-and-a-half drive from the border of the largest Central Asian Republic, Kazakhstan. Someone in Saratov had been writing for months to the headquarters in Moscow asking for The Salvation Army to come to the city. This in itself is not unusual. We get many requests like that. Because it was in my region, headquarters asked me to go and check it out. So I flew there, with just the name of the person who was supposed to meet me.

It was 10.30 on a cold February night when I stepped off the plane and there were two well-dressed men waiting for me. They carried mobile phones and they led me to a new, fully loaded Toyota jeep. If you have a cell phone and a brand new jeep in Russia that usually means you are Mafiya. Things were getting interesting.

I soon realised that my hosts were

pagans in every sense of the word, materialists with seemingly no sense of the transcendent at all. As the jeep started up, our first conversation went like this:

'Geoff,' said Evgeny, 'do you want a cigarette?'

'No thanks, I don't smoke,' I replied.

'Don't smoke, eh?'

'Nope.'

(Pause) 'Do you drink?'

'Nope.'

'Women?'

'Only my wife.'

(Pause) 'Yeah, I've been thinking about giving up smoking too.'

I spent four days being shown around the city by these men, and meeting various people. They took me to a sort of children's home run by the police, but which in reality was a children's prison. In this huge, cavernous building, opened in 1837, the youngest child was six years old and the oldest 16. There were 12-year-old-girls who sold themselves on the highways to long-distance truckers; 10-year-old drug addicts, eight-year-old thieves – and policemen were trying to look after them! I was shown into a room and told, 'There used to be a church in this room in the last century, but we can't find anyone to come and do something. We need something for the kids that's lively, that's interesting.' He was describing a Sunday school program, without having seen one. 'If you would like to come you can do this. You can do what you want,' he said as we left.

Throughout those four days I was baffled as to why these two hoods were interested in hosting The Salvation Army. I tried subtly to let them know that even though I was a foreigner, I was not rich and if the Army came to town they were not going to get any money. I must have said it a hundred times, 'We are not a business.' But I sensed that they listened to me without really understanding.

The evening before I left, as I sat in an apartment on a white leather couch surrounded by expensive European appliances, I bluntly put it to them: 'Evgeny, why have you invited The Salvation Army here? What interest do you have? What's in it for you?'

Something special happened at that moment. Jesus spoke to me through the mouth of a bandit. Evgeny, who I was sure had never seen a Bible let alone read one, looked up into my eyes and said: 'You know, I was in Moscow for a couple of years in the early 90s (pause). I was in prison and you visited me (pause), Yeah, some little old lady from The Salvation Army visited me. So I said to myself, "The Salvation Army is a good organisation. When I get out I am going to do what I can to get The Salvation Army into my city." That's why.'

The question: Should we open The Salvation Army in this city at the request of the Mafiya?

Captain Geoff Ryan[14]

Liverpool United!

In 1984 people who lived in council flats in Liverpool had a problem with cockroaches. Week after week they asked the City Council to deal with the insects, but they were ignored. Finally they decided to take action. They organised a competition to see who had the biggest cockroaches. They all collected them in coffee jars and brought them to the Council Chamber to be judged. In the middle of a debate, the people let out their huge cockroaches and asked the Mayor to judge whose was the biggest. The councillors were very angry, and the people were expelled from the chamber. But next day, men came round to clean up the flats!

Roger Bowen[15]

This God

This God,
Who watches worlds,
Sees my heart.
This careful calculator,
Counting countless millions,
Counts me in.

This artist,
Whose canvas outstretches
Eternity at both ends;
Whose palette out-colours planets,
Paints my portrait.

This lover,
Who dreams in universes,
Dreams of me.

This creator,
Whose breadth of vision spans time
And spawns a cosmos;
Whose woven tapestry of purpose,
More compound than chaos,

Eclipsing complexity,
Rolls out like a highway through history;
Whose heartbeat deafens supernovas:
This father
Kisses me.

This playwright,
Playing
With the deaths and entrances of stars;
Scripting
The end from the beginning;
Knowing
The purpose of the play:
Watches
My feeble audition,
And writes
Me
In.   Gerard Kelly 2001

This is my church...

Kenny Mitchell is a professional DJ who likens the contemporary tools of turntables, CD players, drum machines, samplers and computers to the ancient temple instruments of Israel. Often DJ'ing in the context of 'secular' clubs, Kenny says, 'I'll be praying "OK God, some people here are depressed, some are on a high, some are sick. I want to see freedom and joy and something of your truth come out. You've given me two turntables and a CD player – God do your stuff." And he does.' Kenny describes a recent club night in Osaka, Japan, 'At 3.30am we were still spinning and God just moved through the music. Four people became Christians through conversations they had in the chill-out room. The non-believers wanted a spiritual experience, it was the Christians who were most freaked out.'

References

1 Timothy Yates, Ed, *Mission: An Invitation to God's Future* (Sheffield: Cliff College, 2000)

2 Tom and Christine Sine, *Living on Purpose* (London: Monarch, 2002)

3 Douglas Coupland, *Life after God*, (Scribner, 2002)

4 Os Guinness, *The Call* (Carlisle: Spring Harvest/Authentic publishing, 2001), p7

5 John Piper, *Desiring God* (IVP: 2002), p282

6 Bryant L. Myers, *Walking with the Poor*, (Orbus Books, 1999), p184

7 Ron Sider, *Rich Christians in an Age of Hunger* (London: Hodder and Stoughton, Revised Edition, 1997) pxiv

8 John Simpson, *A Mad World, My Masters* (London: Macmillan, 2000), p87

9 Naomi Klein, *No Logo* (London: Flamingo, 2000), p329

10 Mark Stibbe, *From Orphans to Heirs* (Oxford: BRF, 1999) p35

11 Christopher Wright *Christian Mission and the Old Testament: Matrix or Mismatch?*

12 Clark Pinnock and Robert C. Brow, *Unbounded love* (Wipf & Stock, 2001), p112

13 Lesslie Newbigin, *The open Secret: an Introduction to the Theology of Mission* (Grand Rapids: W.B. Eerdman, 1995), p48

14 Captain Geoff Ryan, *Sowing Dragons: Essays in Neo-Salvationism*, p76

15 Roger Bowen, *So I Send You: A Study Guide to Mission* (SPCK, 1996), p200

PURPOSE applied

Use these six questions to explore the dynamic of PURPOSE in your own life. Where do you see yourself in relation to God's purposes, now and in the future?

● Who are you? Do you have a strong sense of your own identity? Do the things that you do – both in and out of work situations – really reflect who you are? Or is there a 'you' that isn't often seen? If God could bring you to a place where the real you was seen, would you want him to?

● Does the idea of living to serve others appeal to you, or repel you? Is this something you have tried to do in your life? If it became a higher priority for you, how would your life have to change?

● Have you always thought of mission and evangelism as the same basic idea, or do you see a difference? Does the mission of God always result in people becoming Christians (this is an open question)? What expressions of God's mission can you imagine that are not centred on evangelism?

● What does shalom (peace) mean in your life? What aspects of shalom do you already experience, and what aspects do you long for? Picture three different people known to you – neighbours, colleagues, friends. What does shalom mean to them?

● Do you have a sense of God's ultimate purpose for your life? What does it include from your current mix of activities and attributes? What might it exclude? How many steps do you need to take from here to there?

● Who are 'the poor'? How does your life touch on their lives? Do you see ways of giving God's blessing to the poor? Do you want to?

- **PASSION** – I will seek a connection between the deepest passions of my heart and the passion in the heart of God.

- **PLACE** – I will seek to connect with God *in* the place in which I stand, *for* the place to which he is calling me.

- **PURPOSE** – I will look for the connection between the evident purposes of my own life and the purposes of God for my context and culture.

- **POWER** – I will seek to connect my strengths and my weaknesses to the power of God, and seek his transformation in both.

- **PROCESS** – I will connect with the process and pace by which God has worked, is working and will work in my life.

- **PERSPECTIVE** – I will look for the connection between my role in the mission of God and the wider perspective of history, finding my place in God's promise-plan.

POWER

Habit #4 – I will seek to connect my strengths and my weaknesses to the power of God, and seek his transformation in both

 You can do no great things. Only small things with great love.
Mother Theresa

640K ought to be enough for anybody. Bill Gates, 1981

EX. 4:1 Moses answered, 'What if they do not believe me or listen to me and say, "The LORD did not appear to you"?'

2 Then the LORD said to him, 'What is that in your hand?'

'A staff,' he replied.

3 The LORD said, 'Throw it on the ground.'

Moses threw it on the ground and it became a snake, and he ran from it. 4 Then the LORD said to him, 'Reach out your hand and take it by the tail.' So Moses reached out and took hold of the snake and it turned back into a staff in his hand. 5 'This,' said the LORD, 'is so that they may believe that the LORD, the God of their fathers – the God of Abraham, the God of Isaac and the God of Jacob – has appeared to you.'

The story is told of a young monk who arrives at a very old monastery, ready for his first assignment. He is asked to join the assembled brothers who are engaged in making, by hand, painstaking copies of the ancient 'Rule of Life' of the order. He soon notices, however, that they are all making copies of copies – the original manuscript is nowhere to be seen. He wonders at the wisdom of this, and questions the Abbot. Even the smallest error, he points out, will be multiplied and magnified unless the copies are assessed against an original. The Abbot explains that the brothers have been copying from copies for as long as anyone can remember, and that the original manuscript of their Rule of Life is kept locked away in a vault buried deep in the cellars of the monastery.

'But your question is not unwise,' the old man says. 'I will go now and examine the original.'

Taking with him one of the copies from which the men are working, he disappears into the depths of the cellar. Minutes pass, and then hours, but the Abbot does not return.

The young monk becomes concerned, and sets off down the stairs the old man has taken. Before he comes even close to the sacred vault, he hears a loud sobbing echoing through the cellars. Through an open door, he sees the old Abbot holding a dusty manuscript in his hand, banging his head against the wall and crying uncontrollably.

'Why, whatever is the matter, my Father?' the young man asks, and through wracking sobs he hears the Abbot reply: 'the word is *celebrate*.'

In any system of belief and thought passed on from one generation to the next, misunderstandings can be magnified and multiplied. Chinese whispers are far more often the enemy of truth than outright lies. Our grasp on the purposes of God becomes distorted as the story is passed from hand to hand: very often in ways we barely perceive. And there is probably no aspect of the Christian gospel that has suffered more in this way than our understanding of the place of power in our lives. In generation after generation, the global witness of the Christian community has been marred by the hunger for power and by its use and abuse in mission. The claim of Nietzsche that all our motivations are derived from the 'will to power' is hard to justify – just as it is hard to accept Freud's view that it's all about sex or Marx's claim that only economics matter. But there is a grain of truth in each of these assertions, and the drives of money, sex and power assert a strong influence over us.

> Anyone of you knows perfectly well how confused people are, how weak, how many complications and sins have taken root in us. But there is a power which Christ left on earth, which is given to us for free: it is called grace. In Russian the word is *blagodat* – 'the good' (*blago*) which is 'given' (*dat*) for free. You don't have to work for it; it's a gift.
>
> Jenny Robertson

To gain a more balanced view of the workings of power as God intended, we need an original to refer back to – a model that has not been corrupted by centuries of misinterpretation and misuse. The Bible offers a number of such models, and the call of Moses stands out among them. The encounter at the burning bush is, without doubt, an encounter with power. The contrast between the fearful shepherd who begins the conversation and the dynamic leader who comes out of it cannot be explained without reference to power: but this is not a narrative of power in the tradition of comic book heroes. The transformation of Moses by the power of God has features that set it apart from everyday ideas about how power works. God's methods of empowerment are not ours, and there is much to be learned from the 'power dynamic' of Moses' call.

> Injustice occurs when power is misused to take from others what God has given to them, namely their life, dignity, liberty or the fruits of their love and labour.
>
> Gary Haugen[1]

Staff development plan

There are many potential candidates for the accolade 'worst joke in the world', and this may be one of them. Q: What's brown and sticky? A: a stick. It is a simple stick that lies at the heart of Moses' transformation by God's power.

What do YOU have in your hand?

Faced with a challenge and a call that he clearly sees as impossible, Moses asks what he is expected to do if the people of Israel – let alone Pharaoh and his henchmen – don't believe him. God's reply echoes down the centuries as a question to which every believer must respond at some stage in their life: 'What do you have in your hand?' For Moses, the answer is a stick. He is carrying the simple staff that is his trademark as a shepherd – probably roughly carved by his own hand from a carefully chosen tree branch. This is the stick that is transformed by the miraculous power of God and becomes, from that day on, the 'Staff of God'. When Moses and Aaron walk into the presence of Pharaoh at the very epicentre of Egypt's power, it is the staff that they carry with them (Ex. 7:9). When Moses stretches his arm towards the Red Sea, only to watch it divide, the staff of God is in his hand (Ex. 14:16). When the nation of Israel battles the Amalekites and Moses must stand on the hill with his arms raised, it is again the staff of God that he holds (Ex. 17:9). By the end of the adventure, the humble shepherd's staff has had almost as significant a role in the drama as the humble shepherd: it is the central symbol, in the whole Exodus story, of the power of God.

> So Moses took the 'staff of God' (v. 20). What had once been ordinary became extraordinary by virtue of its use in the service of God. So equipped, Moses prepared to return to Egypt.
>
> Expository Bible Commentary[2]

There is significance in God's choice of Moses' staff as an instrument of his power. It was no doubt a convenient prop, and one that Moses always had to hand, but there is more here. The stick represents all that has gone wrong in Moses' life: his poverty, humiliation, failure and fear are all somehow invested in the staff. It speaks of his role as a shepherd, despised in Egypt; of his exile in Midian; of the ashes of a life he must once have hoped would blaze. It speaks of his ordinary working life as an unspectacular peasant herdsman. Yet it is here, at the very point of Moses' weakness, that God chooses to display his

---

WHAT DO YOU HAVE IN YOUR HAND?

The staff was a symbol of Moses' work, of his ordinary life and of the failures he had experienced. If God had to choose a single symbol to represent these things in your life, what would it be? What would the impact of God's anointing on this symbol be?

---

power. There are several lessons to be learned from this dramatic saga of empowerment.

– Firstly, *power in poverty*: the power of God is made manifest in weakness: the power has come, but the weaknesses remain

– Secondly, *power beyond competence*: we are called to live in radical dependence on God's power

– Thirdly, *power in partnership*: God's power transforms our strengths as well as our weaknesses

– Fourthly, *power on purpose*: the power of God will always fulfil the plan of God.

Working Weak

The choice of the shepherd's stick as the instrument of God's power guaranteed, as far as such a thing is possible, that Moses would be 'tooled up' with God's power wherever he went. He would be used to making sure he had his staff with him before working or travelling, and God's power would thus be portable and available. But it also offered a second guarantee: wherever Moses went with the

Staff of God in his hand, he would be reminded of his past. This would not be in an unhealthy or morbid sense, but in the sense that Moses knew his weaknesses and remembered his roots. Moses would be able to sing with Jennifer Lopez in *Jenny from the Block*: 'no matter where I go I still know where I came from'.

> The words we use in trying to communicate the Christian message in the Christian experience have to be charged with strength and power, but they can only be charged with strength and power if they spring from the silence of the Spirit in our inner being ...
>
> John Main[3]

As he stood before Pharaoh, Moses would identify himself by the very carrying of the staff as a failed and a broken man. At every stage, the poignancy of God's victory would be set alongside the sobering reminder of Moses' weaknesses. Carrying a shepherd's staff into Pharaoh's throne room would be like arriving at Royal Ascot in a Robin Reliant, or attending a Gala Première in your shell suit. It was a sign of poverty and humility. Remember those teenage dreams about going to school in your underwear? I have no doubt that this is the kind of exposure Moses would have felt as he approached the Saddam Hussein of his day. He was naked but for the power of God. He was so far out on a limb that the trunk of the tree was a distant blur. God had offered Moses no choice – there was to be no power without poverty; no winning without weakness. Wherever the power of God was displayed, so was the vulnerability of Moses. Nothing extraordinary would take place without Moses being reminded just how ordinary he was. This is an understanding of power unlike any other – the power that is made perfect in weakness.

> The pursuit of Christ is a pilgrimage that involves learning how to give up power for the sake of others. It produces a freedom from fear and anxiety, so that followers can relinquish the need for control.
>
> Mike Riddell

The power of God connects with our lives at the very point of our weakness. In our bankruptcy, God makes his potency known. Miracles are the possibilities that lie deep in the soil of our winter lives, waiting only for the sunshine of God to break out. So why do we devote so much of our time to denying our faults, disguising our failures and distancing ourselves from our all-too-evident frailties? Why do we arrive at Christian meetings hoping above all hope that no one will ask the awkward question and see through to our vulnerability? The walls we build to protect our vulnerable places are

---

STRENGTH TESTS

● What are your greatest strengths? Are any of these in areas you have had little opportunity to explore?

● What are your greatest weaknesses? Can the power of God overcome them?

● If you were offering vocational guidance to someone who had your strengths, your weaknesses, your dreams and your faith, which direction would you point them in?

---

walls that keep out God's power. In God's economy, weakness is the route to power: there is no other.

Dietrich Bonhoeffer gave up his freedom and ultimately his life in resistance to the rise of National Socialism in Hitler's Germany. He could not accept that God's power could be allied to or expressed in the dogma of racial superiority and violence towards the weak. The result was a head-to-head confrontation between a gospel of weakness and love and a system of power and might. In *No Rusty Swords*, Bonhoeffer suggests that Christians can only confront the abuse of power in human culture if they are prepared to accept vulnerability and weakness in their own lives. Meekness, not majesty, should be the defining mark of the community of God. 'We are here and we are joined together not as a community of those who know', he wrote, 'but of those who all look for the word of their Lord and seek everywhere if they cannot hear it; not as those who know, but as those who seek, those who are hungry, those who wait, those who are in need, those who hope.' [4]

Lean on Me

The lesson Moses learned through the 'Staff of God' was one that was central to the whole Exodus adventure, that would remain pertinent for the rest of his life and would later shape the history of Israel significantly. It was this: that the power of God can only truly be experienced in radical dependence. It is when you come to the end of yourself that you touch the beginning of God's power.

> Israel's deliverance from Egypt was not based on human resources. The Israelites had no army; they had no weapons with which to fight; they had no expertise in guerrilla warfare. God was the sole power behind this mission of deliverance.
>
> Gailyn Van Rheenen[5]

God's power did not simply bring out the best in Moses, tapping into inner resources he didn't know he had. The burning bush was not a super-charged one-on-one motivational seminar aimed at 'awakening the giant within'. No amount of positive thinking could transform Moses from a coward-in-exile to a warrior-in-waiting. It took an outside force, the incomparable power of Yahweh, to achieve the transformation. The Exodus is inexplicable without the intervention of God in power. What Moses later put into practice on a national scale, he had learned on a personal scale. When he exhorted the slaves at their most desperate moment to stand firm on God's promise and trust in his power (Ex. 14:13), he was applying the lesson of the staff: that God's power would kick in when his own ran out. Limited to his own resources – or even to the combined potential of the entire slave community – Moses couldn't come close to God's rescue plan. The scale was too great and the need too desperate for humanism. Moses was radically dependent on the power of God. If God did not act, the slaves would die.

Anatoly Emmanuilovich Levitin was a Russian Orthodox believer who, even in old age, was harassed by the KGB. Twice he was imprisoned for his faith – but on each occasion he discovered, in the midst of his loss, the miracle of God's power. Writing from prison, the elderly saint said: 'The greatest miracle of all is prayer. I have only to turn my thoughts to God and I suddenly feel a strength, which bursts into me from somewhere, bursts into my soul, into my entire being. What is it? Psychotherapy? No, it is not psychotherapy, for where would I, an insignificant, tired old man, get this strength which renews me and saves me, lifting me above the earth? It comes from without and there is no force on earth that can even understand it.'[6]

BULLDOZING BLOCKAGES

When you think of connecting with God's purposes, what gets in the way? Are there recurrent blockages? Three of the most likely are unconquered fears, unresolved conflicts and untamed habits. Identify your own besetting weaknesses and ask yourself – what is a realistic time scale to move on from these? Who do you know who can help you?

There is a remarkable correlation between Chapters 13 and 14 of the Exodus story. In Chapter 13 we are told (in verse 18), that 'The Israelites went up out of Egypt armed for battle.' And yet in Chapter 14, when the armies of Pharaoh are bearing down on them, Moses tells them (in verse 14) 'The LORD will fight for you; you need only to be still.' How tempting it must have been to fight. Even with primitive peasant weapons against the best-equipped army in the known world, there would have been a desperate urge to 'go down fighting'. Our inbuilt fight or flight mechanisms are strong, and the instinct towards self-preservation would be overwhelming in such circumstances. But God didn't want a self-preserved people. He wanted a people who would trust him in the future because he had saved them in the past – a people who had faced an enemy as far beyond their competence as walking on the ceiling is beyond a crawling child – and had seen his deliverance first-hand. This event, with men, women and children in fear for their lives, became the turning point in Israel's story. It is here, the narrative tells us, that the people 'feared the LORD and put their trust in him and in Moses his servant' (Ex. 14:31).

The journey beyond competence became the most instructive and nation-shaping event in all history. Faith is born in the waters we dive into when we leave the safe shores of our competence behind.

An ancient prayer attributed to St Cuthbert captures this deep sense of dependence on God – and the importance of the Exodus narrative as an inspiration and example. 'The land is bleak with snow, clouds lour in the sky, there is a gale raging and the sea is a fury of waves, we are dying of hunger and there is no chance of human aid. Then let us storm Heaven with our prayers, asking that the same Lord who parted the Red Sea and fed His people in the desert take pity on us in our peril.'[7]

Sometimes the only part we can play in the battles to which God calls us is to 'storm heaven with our prayers'. But it is in these very times that the power of God is proven. What greater account can there be of the power and providence of God than the human being who says 'I was at my wit's end and utterly desperate – but God heard my cry.' Desperation is not comfortable, but it is the neighbourhood where the power of God hangs out.

Imagine a twenty-ton truck coming towards you on an otherwise empty road. You turn to face it, rooted to the spot. Any moment it will hit you. And then you hear the voice of someone you have learned to love and trust saying, 'Stand still'. What would you do?

RADICAL DEPENDENCE

Have you ever been in a 'Red Sea' situation – the sea ahead of you, Pharaoh's army behind and no chance of getting through without God's help? How did it feel, and what happened? If you haven't had this experience, find someone who has and ask them. If there is a Red Sea between you and God's purposes, what might it be?

The notion of 'comfort zones' is familiar to many people, and we are often exhorted to leave them – but this story introduces the parallel idea of a *competence zone*. My competence zone is the territory within which I know what I'm doing. Its boundaries are the places beyond which the solutions to problems and challenges will not come from me – or not, at least, in any way that I can predict or control. Competence zones affect people in many ways. Some of us are afraid to leave our own country, because language is a key thread of our competence. Others of us seek to manage our homes and jobs in such a way that competence boundaries are never crossed. Powerful people often use their power defensively, to ensure that they remain within their self-identified competence zone. Had Moses done this, the slaves would never have been freed. Worse still, they might have been annihilated. Moses was radically dependent on God because he was so utterly and inarguably beyond his own competence zone – and he knew it. His life teaches us that the richest experiences of God's power lie, by definition, in the lands beyond my competence zone. If too few of us in contemporary culture are experiencing the power of God, it may just be because too many of us are afraid to leave our competence zones.

John Piper suggests that 'God is not looking for people who will work for him, so much as he is looking for people who will let him work for them.' God's power does not draw alongside me to complement and complete my own skills, like cream added to coffee or sugar to a bowl of cornflakes. It is not the icing on the cake of my performance. It comes to me from outside, making performance possible when I am so far outside my competence zone that I'm not sure I'll ever get back in. God gets the credit when no other source can explain my survival and success.

The power is within you.

#1 misconception of the contemporary world.

Strength to serve

Having established that the doorway to God's power lies beyond our competence zone, the narrative doubles back on itself. God's question to Moses, 'What do you have in your hand?' and the later unfolding of the adventure contain a surprise. Moses will only know the power of God when he moves out of range of his own strengths: but that does not mean that those strengths will lie unused. God overcomes Moses' weaknesses, but he also transforms and uses his strengths. Moses discovers the central lesson of trust; that once he is willing to step out of his competence zone, his competencies are restored to him. There are elements in Moses' character and personality, in his human gifting and in his experience that fit him uniquely for the task to which God calls him. God's anointing of Moses for the task does not begin with his call but with his birth; his reliance on supernatural gifting does not negate the use of his natural gifts. God takes both the weaknesses and the strengths of Moses and shapes both for his purposes.

> **It is the duty of a good shepherd to shear his sheep, not to skin them.**
>
> Tiberius Caesar, 42BC-AD37

God does not reduce us to nothing, he makes us into something. Before he calls us out, he stands us up. It is a common mistake amongst God's people to assume that the statement 'I need God' must always be allied to the statement

---

THE DOCTOR IS IN

When people e-mail you or speak to you and ask for your help or advice, what is the one area they are most often seeking help in?

'God does not need me.' We are so convinced, rightly, of the power and sovereignty of God that we cannot bring ourselves to say 'God needs me.' But he does. He needs me not because he is forced to need me but because he has chosen to. He invites me to enter into a partnership in which his strength and my strengths work together. I am called to be radically dependent on his power – to know that without his intervention I cannot do the things he has called me to do – but I am called in such a way that my strengths have their finest hour. God asks me 'what do you have in your hand?' because the things I carry can be taken up and used in his service. I come to him in weakness, but he looks also to deploy my strengths. To believe that I have everything I need without God is pure folly: but to believe that I am nothing; that I bring no gifts to the partnership is equally mistaken.

Definition: MANIPUPHOBIA – fear of gaining, exercising or enjoying power in case it leads to abuse. A common characteristic of Generation X, producing a reluctance to engage in decision-making and to take responsibility.

'In other words,' Os Guinness writes, 'there is more to God's call than simply sending us out – the commissioning, as calling is usually thought to be. Certainly, it ends by "sending us out", but it begins by "singling us out" – we are called by name – and it continues by "standing us up". As we respond to the call of our Creator, we rise to our feet, not only physically but also in every sense of the word, to be the people he alone knows we are capable of being.'[9]

> We are all dependent on God, whether we acknowledge this fact or not. For centuries contemplatives have opened their day with the prayer, 'Thank you, O God, for waking me this morning. You didn't have to.'
>
> Bryant L. Myers

The call of Bezalel and Oholiab in Exodus 36-38 to help Moses with the creation and furnishing of the tabernacle beautifully illustrates God's refusal to reject 'natural' gifting. These men are artists and craftsmen, with skills that they have honed over years of learning, development and practice – and yet they are described as filled with God's Spirit. God wants (aka needs) their every gift to make the worship of the people of Israel deep and real. We are told of Bezalel that God had 'filled him with the Spirit of God, with skill, ability and knowledge in all kinds of crafts.' (Ex. 35:31)

Terence Fretheim writes:

> Bezalel executes in miniature the divine creative role of Genesis 1 in the building of the tabernacle. The spirit of God with which the craftsmen are filled is a sign of the living, breathing force that lies behind the completing of the project just as it lies behind the creation. Their intricate craftsmanship mirrors God's own work. The precious metals with which they work take up the very products of God's beautiful creation and give new shape to that beauty within the creation ... The importance given to shape, order, design, intricacy – for example, the embroidery (36:37; 38:18) – and the visual aspect, including colour (36:8; 35; 38:18-23), in both structure and furnishings, corresponds with the orderly, colourful, artful, and intricate creation of Genesis 1.[10]

If weakness is the doorway into the experience of God's power, strength is what we find when we get there. God takes all that we are and invites us to partner with him in the adventure of worship and redemption. We are not sleeping partners, passively receiving his power like computers waiting for the programmer's command: we are active and intelligent human beings called to bring all that we are into the partnership of power. God chooses us and God uses us. Both our weaknesses and our strengths are taken up into his power and love, and transformed as we embrace his purposes for our lives.

Living on purpose

Lastly, Moses discovers that God's power will also move towards the fulfilment of God's plan. Moses had to step out of his competence zone to discover the power of God and what he stepped into was obedience. There can be no question of seeking power for power's sake, nor for its experiential buzz. Nor is Moses being built up so that he can look in the mirror and bask in the power and pride displayed there. God is raising him up for a purpose, and it is as he steps into that purpose that the power flows.

Do you long to know more of the power of God? Engage more fully with the purposes of God. Do you crave a life that resonates with the infilling of power? Seek a life that is marked by the outpouring of love. Are you looking for technique that will switch on the power of God in your experience? Look for opportunities to plug in to the mission of God.

If God has made his power available for the fulfilment of his purposes, it follows that the place to be if you want to know his power is the centre of his will. The more you understand the purposes of God, the more you are able to put yourself into situations in which you experience the power of God. Are you tired of going to the front of the meeting to seek God's power? Try going to the end of the street to find his mission.

The God of the burning bush is engaged in a cosmic struggle with the forces of death and darkness that have marred and disfigured his creation. He fights injustice and oppression, exploitation and greed and all that stands against his promise of shalom. Moses discovered the reality of the power of God when he, too, stepped into this struggle. Like a new recruit passing through the quartermaster's stores, it was as he volunteered for active duty that the tools and weaponry he needed were issued to him. Don't wait until you have the power of God to find his purpose. Seek his purpose, step out, and the power will come.

> I tell our staff that Christian ministers are people who get their strength from God, go into the world and get bashed around. Then we come back, get our strength from God, go back into the world, get bashed around. And that is our life. We go, get bashed, get strength, go, get bashed, get strength. And we *can* take on strength in this way.'
>
> Ajith Fernando[11]

BURDENS AND BONDAGES

Picture yourself walking into the room you are now in, but carrying a heavy backpack. It is really weighing you down. As you take it off your back, you see that it is full of bricks. It is a huge relief to put the heavy pack down. As you remove the bricks, you see that they are labelled. What words do you see written on them?

Do or don't do. There is no try.

Yoda

Invitation to the Feast

Come, all you who thirst,
   all you who hunger for the bread of
   life,
   all you whose souls cry out for
   healing;
Come, come to the feast of life.

Come, all you who are weary,
   all you who are bowed down with
   worry,
   all you who ache with the tiredness
   of living;
Come, come to the feast of life.

Come, all you poor,
   all you who are without food or
   refuge,
   all you who go hungry in a fat land;
Come, come to the feast of life.

Come, all you who are bitter,
   all you whose hopes have tarnished
   into cynicism,
   all you who feel betrayed and
   cannot forgive;
Come, come to the feast of life.

Come, all you who grieve,
   all you who suffer loss as a fresh
   knife wound,
   all you who curse the God you love;
Come, come to the feast of life.

Come, all you who are sinners,
   all you who have sold the gift that is
   within you,
   all you who toss uneasily in your bed

   at night;
Come, come to the feast of life.

Come, all you who are oppressed,
   all you who have forgotten the
   meaning of freedom,
   all you who cry out to the very heart
   of God;
Come, come to the feast of life.

Come, all you who are traitors,
   all you who use your wealth and
   power to crucify God,
   all you who cannot help yourselves;
Come, come to the feast of life.

Come, all you who are sick,
   all you whose bodies or minds have
   failed you,
   all you who long above all for
   healing;
Come, come to the feast of life.

Come, all you who are lost,
   all you who search for meaning but
   cannot find it,
   all you who have no place of
   belonging;
Come, come to the feast of life.

The table of Jesus is your place of
gathering
   here you are welcomed, wanted,
   loved,
   here there is a place set for you;
Come, come to the feast of life.

Mike Riddell [12]

POWER applied

Use these six questions to explore the dynamic of 'power' in your own life. Where do you see yourself in relation God's power in your life?

● Do you find power attractive, or frightening? Looking at Christian history, do you see power as a corrupting influence, or a helpful one – or both?

● What do you have in your hand? If God was looking for a symbol of your ordinariness – perhaps including your weaknesses and failures – what symbol could he choose? What would it mean to you if this became the symbol of God's power?

● Have you ever been in a situation of total dependence on God – where all is lost unless a prayer in answered? What emotions did you go through? How did the outcome impact your faith? If you have never been in such a situation, how do you think you might react?

● Which do you think will help the poor more – refusing to take power because you have no right to it, or taking power and trying to use it to their advantage (this is an open question)? How do you handle power?

● Can you see ways in which you could, from where you stand, step into God's power by stepping into his mission?

● Do your weaknesses frustrate you? Can you envisage finding a place in God's purposes but still carrying them with you? What would the implications be?

References

1 Gary Haugen, *Good News About Injustice* (IVP, 1999), p72

2 *The Expositor's Bible Commentary*, Zondervan, 1989-1999, CD Rom version

3 Richard J. Foster and Emilie Griffin, *Spiritual Classics: reading with the heart*, (Fount, 1999), p179

4 Dietrich Bonhoeffer, *No Rusty Swords* (Fontana, 1970)

5 Gailyn Van Rheenen, *Missions: Biblical Foundations and Contemporary Strategies* (Zondervan, 1996), p17

6 Jenny Robertson, *Windows to Eternity* (Oxford: Bible Reading Fellowship), p28

7 Bede, *The Life of Cuthbert*, cited in Michael Mitton, *Restoring the Woven Cord* (Darton, Longman and Todd, 1995), p129

8 Dietrich Bonhoeffer, *No Rusty Swords*

9 Os Guinness, *The Call* (Carlisle: Spring Harvest Publishing, 2001), p84

10 Terence Fretheim, *Interpretation: Exodus* (Westminster John Knox Press, 1991), p269, 270

11 Ajith Fernando, *Missionaries for the right reasons*, Conference presentation, 2000

12 Quoted in Pete Ward, Ed., *Mass Culture: Eucharist and Mission in a Post-Modern World* (Oxford: Bible Reading Fellowship, 1999), p103

- **PASSION** – I will seek a connection between the deepest passions of my heart and the passion in the heart of God.

- **PLACE** – I will seek to connect with God *in* the place in which I stand, *for* the place to which he is calling me.

- **PURPOSE** – I will look for the connection between the evident purposes of my own life and the purposes of God for my context and culture.

- **POWER** – I will seek to connect my strengths and my weaknesses to the power of God, and seek his transformation in both.

- **PROCESS – I will connect with the process and pace by which God has worked, is working and will work in my life.**

- **PERSPECTIVE** – I will look for the connection between my role in the mission of God and the wider perspective of history, finding my place in God's promise-plan.

PROCESS

Habit #5 – I will connect with the process and pace by which God has worked, is working and will work in my life

> " When I was young I used to hate going to weddings because my ageing aunts would poke me in the ribs and say "You're next". They stopped doing it the day I started going to funerals and poking them. Anon
>
> **If you are going through hell, keep going.** Winston Churchill "

EX. 6 Then he said, 'I am the God of your father, the God of Abraham, the God of Isaac and the God of Jacob.' At this, Moses hid his face, because he was afraid to look at God. ...

11 But Moses said to God, 'Who am I, that I should go to Pharaoh and bring the Israelites out of Egypt?' 12 And God said, 'I will be with you. And this will be the sign to you that it is I who have sent you: When you have brought the people out of Egypt, you will worship God on this mountain.'

I discovered something new about myself recently – or at least a new way of explaining things – and it is surprising how much difference it makes. The discovery began over lunch with a US-based expert on missions named David Pollock. David was able to make several observations about my life with uncanny accuracy. When I commented on this, he said, 'Of course – you're a third culture kid.'

This was not a description I had ever used of myself – but the more I explored its meaning, the more accurate it seemed. 'TCK's' are those who spend a significant part of their developing years – 0 to 18 – in a culture or cultures other than their parents' home culture. I had heard the phrase used often of the children of missionaries – and had worked with a number over the years – but for some reason I had never applied the same analysis to my own situation. Having now read David Pollock's excellent book on the subject, *Third Culture Kids – The Experience of Growing up Among Worlds*, I am amazed that I have lived for so long without knowing who I am.[1]

When I reviewed my own history in the course of reading the book, I established that by the time I was eleven years old, I had lived at nine different addresses in four countries on two continents. I had attended eight different schools and learned grammar, history and geography from an Irish, Canadian, French and British perspective, and I had been introduced to so many different team sports that I simply gave up trying. Like many TCK's, I have tended to 'bury' many memories and experiences because they have little value or currency in 'home' culture. The characteristics of adult TCK's can be both positive and negative, but common traits include restlessness, frequent job/location changes and a pervading sense of not having any one place to call 'home'. TCK's are often strong leaders, but are also often emotionally unsettled – sometimes decades after they have 'settled' in one culture.

Exploring the TCK profile has been, for me, a question of understanding things about myself that I have barely been aware of for some twenty-five adult years. The fuzzy impressions have been there, but not the focus. Others will have a very different life-experience – but it occurs to me that the principle may be the same. We are so busy growing up and getting on with our lives that we rarely take the time to reflect on who we are and who we are becoming. Moses was in his eighties when God called him out of obscurity into the glaring spotlight of conflict with Pharaoh – but as a result he was able to understand his own past, present and future in the light of God's plans. As the narrative unfolds, we see a man who is able to let go of fears, insecurities and anxieties in the certain knowledge that God has been at work, is at work and will be at work in his life. Moses encounters the passion, power and purpose of God: but he also comes to a deeper understanding of process.

Definition: ECHOPHOBIA – fear of moving forward into the future because the echo of past events always haunts you. Can only be treated by naming the shadows and claiming God's light.

Few of us can afford the luxury of halting everything to 'find ourselves', and the cry 'stop the world, I want to get off' has always fallen on deaf ears. But we may be able to make time and space to reflect – perhaps to review our own history, to get some help from those who understand our experiences, and to come to a clearer and stronger view of 'who we are'. We will be better people for it, and perhaps better able to respond to God's call on *our* lives. It is an inherent feature of God's call on our lives that it throws light:

■ **On the hand of God in our past**: we are brought into a deeper understanding of the *patience* of God's work in our lives.

■ **On the rhythms of God in our present**: we come to appreciate the *pace* of God's work in our lives.

BUMP-STARTING THE PROCESS

Think back over the last twelve to twenty-four months of your life. Think about your spirituality and lifestyle, and your 'connectedness' to God's mission. Are there things that were happening that no longer are? Did you begin to embrace certain changes, only to let them slip? Are there processes of God's work that have stalled in your life? If so, what might you be able to do to re-start them?

■ **On the plans of God for our future**: we build on the certainty of the *promise* of God's work in our lives.

Each of these three is, in its own way, a liberation. We are set free from the bondages of the past, from captivity to the present and from fear of the future. Only out of such freedom are we able to move forward, step by step, in the path God has set out for us. There is a confidence that comes from knowing that the God who calls us today has cared for us yesterday and will continue with us tomorrow. This is the anchor that makes adventure possible, the certainty that feeds our courage.

We will fail to benefit from the certainty of God's presence and promise if we focus only on immediate expectations. The global search for an alternative to the petrol-based internal combustion engine has met with varying degrees of success. More often than not, the attitude that sets the search back is an over-emphasis on the immediate. The usefulness of oil as a fuel, for example, is hard to deny. Cars that run on petrol or diesel have been shown to be faster, more powerful, more efficient and

more flexible than any of the alternatives. Electric cars are slow and can rarely cover more than fifty to a hundred miles without a re-charge. Alternative fuels are expensive and complex to use, and usually impair performance. If all that matters is a car that runs from A to B in the fastest possible time and at the lowest cost, oil-based fuels win every time. So why are so many scientists worldwide engaged in the search for alternatives? Because they look at oil not only in terms of the 'now moment' of combustion, but also in terms of its past – where it comes from and how it gets to the point of combustion – and in terms of its future: what happens after combustion. So it is with questions of supply (when will the oil run out?) and of pollution (will car exhausts poison the world?) that research concerns itself. An analysis based only on the moment produces a distorted result – it is only as both the past and the future are considered that a balanced view is taken.

Moses discovered that the God with whom he is called to do business at Horeb is a God who has already taken account of his past and future. It is only as he recognises this, and accepts God's analysis of both, that he is able to step into his purpose in God's mission. God looks for us to connect not only with what he is doing in our lives today, but also with what he has done and will do.

God in my past – The hidden thread of grace

God spoke to me about his hand at work in my past in a remarkable way in 1995. We had returned as a family from missionary service in France, having moved from the UK two years earlier utterly convinced that God had called us to go and would keep us there. The fact that we had no choice but to return to the UK was confusing, humiliating and unsettling. We had neither jobs nor a home to come back to – everything had been staked on a long-term call to France. I found myself plunged into an intense period of self-examination and re-evaluation. In the middle of this cloud of confusion, within a few weeks of our return, my mother died. Her death was totally unexpected, and hit me hard. I found myself asking where God could possibly be in all this. I grieved for my mother, who had separated from my father in 1970 after nineteen years of marriage, and had been unable to speak a single word to him since. I thought of all the many difficult things I had lived through in my childhood and wondered where was God then? I thought of the mixed messages and conflicting emotions I had received through my family line: the

hurts and half-truths I was still, in adulthood, fighting to overcome. The plans I had staked my life on had failed me. The hopes I had nurtured for my future were gone.

It is easy to look back and see this as a storm in a teacup – but when you're in the bottom of the cup and the leaves are swirling around you, the storm is real and alarming. Your world folds in on itself and the rim of the teacup is about as wide a horizon as you can take in. I lost sight of God in the churning clouds of the immediate. I found him again in a National Trust bookshop.

We had been offered the opportunity of a quiet weekend at a friend's cottage in Norfolk, and leapt at the chance. Browsing in the souvenir shop of a stately home, I came across a postcard bearing the traditional crest of the Kelly family. I had known the crest from my earliest childhood, when my father had told stories – barely believable even then – of our descent from the thirteenth-century kings of Ireland. What I had not known though, and discovered now, was that we also have an ancient family motto. It is *turris fortis mihi Deus* – 'God is a strong tower to me.' The discovery of these words hit me like thunder – not only because they reminded me that my strength was in God, but for a much deeper reason. In an instant I understood that my family, centuries before my birth, had committed themselves to the God I so desperately needed to find again.

THE HIDDEN THREAD OF GRACE

On a large sheet of paper, draw the story of your life as a road or river. Use words and pictures to represent key moments and milestones. If you are in a group setting, tell someone else your story using these words and pictures. As you look at the story, do you see evidence of a 'hidden thread of grace', God's working in your life?

In the mists of ancient Celtic history, the family from whom I draw my name and my heritage had chosen to identify themselves by their dependence on God. I was confused by God's apparent absence from my life on a scale of weeks. God was affirming his presence in my life over centuries.

It is hard to capture just how important this discovery was to me. For a whole host of reasons, I had never seen my family line as a source of encouragement in my faith. Like Moses, I found it hard to see the hand of God in the things that had happened to me, or in the worldview into which I had been born and raised. But here was God assuring me that he was 'the God of my fathers'; that centuries before my birth he had been at work in the Kelly tribe. I saw in an instant how small I am, how great God is and yet how infinitely he cares for me.

The tidal wave that knocked Moses off his feet and landed him in an entirely new place before God came in part from this realisation – that *this* God was the God of his fathers; that there was continuity of care; that he, Moses, was one link in a chain established centuries before his birth. We know that this caused Moses to stop and reflect on his personal history because later, when he came to tell the story of his life to others, he included the incidents recorded in the first two chapters of the Exodus story. Here was the miracle of God working through a team of midwives who risk their own lives to save male children from death; here is the mother of Moses inspired to commit him to the safety of a reed boat; here is the daughter of Pharaoh finding him; here is her father allowing the child to be brought up in the palace and offering the education and training that would in due course cause his empire to tremble. These stories are recorded for us because they tell of the remarkable thread of grace that runs through Moses' early life; of the invisible hand of God at work.

We do not know if Moses, before the call of God at Horeb, was aware of the significance of these events. Judging by his early responses to God's call, it seems unlikely. But there is no doubt, as God reveals his character and power, that Moses comes to see the astounding continuity of care that has surrounded him.

It is impossible to come to a mature understanding of the call of God in our lives without this realisation of his hand in our past. The thread of grace is there if we will only find it: and this is the context in which God's call today makes sense.

In the world of TV advertising this same disparity of scale exists. Watching a thirty second commercial, it is easy to be caught up in the creativity of the moment and to think only of the now – but those thirty seconds are the visible tip of an iceberg of process lying under the surface. In even a basic commercial, the journey from the initial concept or idea to the finished event is convoluted. The idea is developed and explored. Once it is refined, a script must be commissioned and agreed. The script then goes into research to ensure that the right message is being communicated. The dialogue, actors, extras and camera moves are rehearsed for several days. The lighting will be perfected over a couple of days to create the right atmosphere. 'Experts' will be brought to advise on specifics and details of the story. On the day of the shoot, thirty-plus people will be around to make sure everything goes smoothly, from make-up to camera tracking and even then, at the end of the day, if the director isn't happy he'll shout 'cut!' and they'll do it all over again. The phrase 'that's a wrap' is always hard won and never unappreciated. The result: a TV commercial or film that is technically and visually perfect. The journey: at least four weeks of research, writing, storyboarding, rehearsing and shooting. This gives a ratio of preparation to performance for a thirty second commercial of 80,640 to 1.

Hardly surprising, then, that God was prepared to put four centuries into planning the liberation of the Hebrew slaves, or eighty years into preparing Moses for his call. 'Here we see God at work; silently at first, equipping Moses with those skills and abilities which will later be required of him and will help make him the great deliverer of God's people', Stephen Dray writes in *Exodus – Free to Serve*. 'It will nevertheless be nearly 80 years before God is ready to act. God's time-scale is rarely ours and we can often be deceived into thinking that he is inactive, even unconcerned. Yet God is working all the time, unseen by us.'[2]

The call at Shepherd's Bush is not the first note of God's work in Moses' life. It is the culmination of a grand scheme: like a single note standing out from a symphony. As Os Guinness remarks, God is at work 'Like a coach bringing out the full capacity of each member of the team, or a conductor bringing out the deepest potential of the orchestra. God's call resonates in us at depths no other call can reach and draws us on and out and up to heights no other call can scale or see.'[3]

Your experience may be utterly unlike that of Moses. But what does it mean to you to see and celebrate the continuity of God's care in your life? How does it change your view of God's call to know that the threads of his plans for you began to be spun centuries before your birth, and that from your first breath he has watched over you, willing and wooing you towards the centre of his love? God's self-proclamation to Moses, 'I am what I am', might loosely be paraphrased 'I wasn't born yesterday'. How does it impact you to know that the God who calls you didn't arrive on today's boat – but has been there all along?

I wrote this poem in 1988, at a time when God was bringing waves of healing to the hurts in my life. The title came later, courtesy of Leonardo DiCaprio.

King of the World

Lord, my heart is like an iceberg.
Not cold and hard
But seven-tenths hidden.
If I love you only
With the parts that show
My love won't last the course,
But if I am to love you
With my whole heart
I must face the pain
Of hidden things
Surfacing.

Come, Lord
With the Titanic of your love
Collide with my heart
And in that great collision
Let it be
My reservations
That sink forever.

God in my present – love at three miles an hour

Kosuke Koyama was a Japanese theologian who served as a missionary pastor in Thailand. Working amongst simple peasants and rice-farmers, he came to two conclusions that were to shape his beliefs and writings. The first was that the lifestyle of the Thai farmers was entirely different to that of the urban Europeans by whom much contemporary theology was being produced. European culture was fast-paced and goal-driven, seeking to dominate and change the world through technology and power. Thai culture, by contrast, was slow, reflective and accepting; shaped by the rhythms of the land, seasons and climate. It was an entirely different culture and context for the mission of God. The second conclusion Koyama reached was that, of these two cultures, it was the Thai experience that was closer to the worldview and ethos of the biblical narrative. He saw individuals, families and communities in the pages of the Bible whose experience was markedly similar to that of the farmers amongst whom he lived and ministered.

Koyama was inspired to explore more deeply the slow-paced unfolding of the biblical story, and especially of the Exodus narrative. Here he found a God who journeyed with his people across the desert as they travelled on foot, never exceeding walking pace. It is unlikely that they ever exceeded three miles an hour, and on a hard day they would average even less. This led him to make the unique observation that the speed of God's love is walking pace – three miles an hour. 'God walks "slowly"', he wrote in 1979, 'because he is love ... Love has its speed. It is an inner speed. It is a spiritual speed. It is a different kind of speed from the technological speed to which we are accustomed ... It goes on in the depth of our life, whether we notice or not, whether we are currently hit by storm or not, at three miles an hour. It is the speed we walk and therefore it is the speed the love of God walks.'[4]

Koyama's work was a necessary corrective to the 'culture of immediacy' that had come to dominate Christian thought and practice in the west. For that reason, it remains a vital and relevant contribution to theology. There is a deep and virulent temptation in the contemporary world to look for fast solutions and a resulting reluctance to engage with the slower pace of God's work. Moses was called to engage in some fairly immediate tasks. Things moved fast once the call had been accepted, and in a flash he was on his way back to Egypt to engage in a conflict that would escalate over a relatively short period of time. But he was also called to be patient. A few weeks of hectic havoc gave way to forty years of walking-pace wanderings. Moses had to build community and create worship in this slower context of uncertainty and frustration. He learned obedience both in the flash-fire of supernatural conflict with the magicians of Egypt *and* in the long haul of nation-forming on dry, hard ground. There were seasons of intense activity, and seasons of waiting on God. Moses' own heart had to be shaped and renewed as he journeyed with God, and there were lessons for the people to learn that only walking pace could offer them. There was visible crisis, but there was also a hidden iceberg of process.

Accepting the pace at which God works in our lives is not easy, and a resistance to the slow turning of God's call can be a cause of personal confusion. Author John Noble often says that he has met many people who are right about the task that God has called them to, but wrong about the timing. We correctly discern God's 'what' but fail to hear his 'when'. There is a now-but-not-yet dimension to all of God's work, and the journey between the two is set at walking pace. There is a principle known in management circles as 'the pregnancy principle'. This states that whilst it takes one woman nine months to produce a baby, you cannot achieve the same result with nine women in one month. Try finding a space that you look at often – a pin-board or picture frame; your bathroom mirror or the fridge door. Take a post-it note or scrap of paper and draw on it three times the capital letter 'T'. Every time you look at it, remember: 'TTT', things take time.

If you are unsure or unaware of God's work in your life, might the reason be that you are applying expectations of

PACEMAKERS

Reflect on the pace of God's work in your life. Is he too fast for you, or too slow? Are there long-term processes of change that he is working on that you have failed to notice: whether by accident or by choice? If you have been running, how might your life change if you walked for a while?

immediacy to a project that is built on a much longer scale? Might you be missing God because you are looking for speed and power while he is at work in gentleness and slow persistence? If you could tune in to this more sensitive register of a work of transformation that doesn't blast you into pieces but walks with you, changing you one step at a time, what do you think you might see of God's well-paced work in your life? What has his whisper been saying while you have been craning for his shout? Carlo Carretto, who left a busy and prestigious post in the Vatican to take up the contemplative life amongst the North African poor, said this, 'God does not hurry over things; time is his, not mine, and I, little creature, have been called to be transformed into God by sharing his life. And what transforms me is the charity which he pours into my heart. Love transforms me slowly into God.'

Four principles govern the period during which Moses led the people of God

through the desert. The freed slaves were called to:

- Worship in the wilderness
- Trust God through the trials
- Find strength in community
- Press on to the promise.

The same four principles are at work in our lives today. There will be 'high and heavy' moments of revelation and anointing; there will be periods of weeks, months or perhaps years when everything is moving and the power of God seems to flow without let or hindrance. But for all of us, without exception, there will be wilderness wanderings. For many the desert times outnumber a hundred times over the high spots of God's revealed activity. And it is in these times that we discover the reality and reliability of faith.

■ Will we continue to worship our God even though we see wilderness to the furthest horizon? The very best tabernacles are those built in desert times.

■ Will our trust in him stay strong in the trials of hunger, poverty, sickness, opposition and misunderstanding; and when our plans seems to be irretrievably stalled? The very richest experiences of God's love and care emerge when times are tough.

■ Will we find pockets of strength in the community that travels with us, and support one another when fantasy is more

---

WHO DO YOU HAVE IN YOUR LIFE?

Identify and make a list of the top three people in your life, who leave you feeling stimulated, challenged and 'moved forward' whenever you spend time with them.

---

attractive than faith? The most fruitful relationships are those forged in shared privations.

■ Will we continue to work towards God's plans and promises for our lives, even though progress is slow and the going hard? The deepest channels in the river of faith are those that run where God has all but disappeared from our lives – and yet we believe.

Our answers to these questions will determine, in large measure, whether we ever get through the desert to the possibilities beyond.

Identify someone in your own experience who has, to your knowledge, experienced the joy and fulfilment of connecting with God's purposes in their lives. Take time out to ask them how they got there. I have no doubt they will speak of high moments of certainty and strength. Almost certainly, they will tell a story in which these high-points of connection stretch across the years like pylons across a vast and open plain. But in between the pylons they will tell you of the weeks, and months, and sometimes years of heavy weather. Desert times are as certain in the purposes of God as nightfall in the turning of the world. Don't fear such times –

walk through them with the God who walks at your side, at three miles an hour.

God in my future – the certainty of things spoken

There is an intriguing cameo within the call of Moses that is found in Exodus 3:12. God has revealed to his potential servant the breadth and splendour of his plan, but Moses is wracked with doubt. Like a pinball machine on a bonus round, his doubts are flashing and ringing on every side. He is afraid of Pharaoh, afraid of the Hebrew slaves and afraid of his own inability – and on each count, he has good reason. What will convince the old shepherd to take the challenge? God's response is to turn a statement of potential into a statement of certainty. The sign of his presence for Moses will be that 'When you have brought the people out of Egypt, you will worship God on this mountain.' There is no 'if' in the sentence – only 'when'.

This best manager in the world couldn't come up with a better motivational matrix. God sees Moses' doubts and invites him to lean on HIS certainties. 'You may doubt that this is possible,' he is saying, 'but I see it as a certainty. I know that you will achieve this task as surely as I know that the sun will rise tomorrow.' Like a parent reassuring a nervous child, like a coach calming his star athlete, God creates a platform of certainty and invites Moses to stand on it. This is significant in the conversation for two reasons.

Firstly, it gives Moses permission to doubt. As long as Moses feels that he can only *do* this thing if he utterly *believes* it to be possible, he is lost. His faith is simply not enough to carry him. There are too many reasons for doubt and fear. God is asking him to bring his doubts along with him, and let the unfolding of events deal with them. Even if I don't believe in God's plans for my life, he believes in them enough for both of us. We know from later events that Moses did overcome his doubts – but at this early stage his faith is fragile. 'Your faith is not strong enough to stand on,' God says to him. 'Stand on mine.' When you cannot find the strength to believe in yourself, hold on to this: God believes in you.

Secondly, and by implication, God's promise gives Moses something to hold on to. The promise not only points to the possibility of freedom, but to its measure. The slavery of the Hebrews is marked and measured by their inability to worship. Not only are they prevented from celebrating the work of God in their lives, but their sweated labour is, by definition, building the reputation of the false gods of Egypt. They are engaged in the grand projects that will tell the world of the greatness of Pharaoh and his gods: they are unwilling servants at the shrines of idols. God gives to Moses a tantalising vision of freedom. The people will be free to worship their God. This vision, of the Hebrew slaves leaving their chains to gather for the worship of Yahweh, fires Moses' imagination. 'In your freedom, you will find the strength to worship – and by your worship you will know how free you are.'

God places before Moses a vision of the future so compelling, so *right*, that the old man can but wonder, and join in. The pattern thus established continues throughout the Old Testament and into the New. The plan of God always moved towards the promise of God. Threads of the story are always written in the future tense. The future is a bookend on the work of God without which the present collapses. If we are to connect with God's purposes today, we need a deep and resonating sense of his tomorrow. Biblical prophecy is never about prediction for prediction' sake – there is no Mystic Meg in God's tool-kit. Prophecy, rather, is about imagining and articulating God's promised future. It is about tapping into the energy and inspiration of his astounding promise-plan, and pulling tomorrow into today. The church, Jurgen Moltmann has said, 'is an arrow sent into the world to point to the future.'

We may not see the road immediately ahead. We may know little of what will come from the commitments God has called us to. But we trust because the far

Do you know what the most frequent command in the Bible turns out to be? What instruction, what order, is given, again and again, by God, by angels, by Jesus, by prophets and apostles? What do you think – 'Be good'? 'Be holy, for I am holy'? Or, negatively, 'Don't sin'? 'Don't be immoral'? No. The most frequent command in the Bible is 'Don't be afraid.' Don't be afraid. Fear not. Don't be afraid.

N.T. Wright[5]

horizons of the future have been set for us. We know that God has the end already in view, and that his promises are sure. Therefore we are able to trust. Even in lostness, we know that God is taking us towards the future he has promised.

> My Lord God, I have no idea where I am going. I do not see the road ahead of me. I cannot know for certain where it will end. Nor do I really know myself, and the fact that I think I am following Your will does not mean that I am actually doing so. But I believe that the desire to please You does in fact please You. And I hope I have that desire for all that I am doing. I hope that I will never do anything apart from that desire. And I know that if I do this You will lead me by the right road, though I may know nothing about it. Therefore I will trust You always though I may seem to be lost and in the shadow of death. I will not fear, for You are ever with me, and You will never leave me to face my perils alone.

Thomas Merton[6]

THE READING CORNER

If you struggle to see where it is that you fit in all that God is doing in the world, try reading a good book on mission. *On Call* by Stuart Buchanan is helpful on calling and vocation, *Upwardly Mobile* by Dave Westlake is excellent on justice and the poor, and *Connect!* by Tim Jeffrey and Steve Chalke offers valuable insights into the shape of God's mission in a changing world.

References

1 David Pollock and Ruth E. van Reken, *Third Culture Kids – The Experience of Growing up among Worlds* (Intercultural Press, 2001)

2 Stephen Dray, *Exodus – Free to Serve*, p23

3 Os Guinness, *The Call*, p84

4 Kosuke Koyama, *Three Mile an Hour God*, (SCM Press, 1979)

5 N.T. Wright, *Following Jesus: Biblical Reflections on Discipleship* (SPCK, 1994), p56

6 Thomas Merton, cited in John Moses, *The Desert* (Norwich: Canterbury Press, 1996) p69

PROCESS applied

Use these six questions to explore the dynamic of 'process' in your own life. Where do you see yourself in relation to God's pace and processes in your life?

● What is there in your past that still shapes your life – positively and negatively – today? How can the good be harnessed and the bad be overcome in God's mission?

● Do you find God's work in your life too slow, or too fast? Are you frustrated with waiting, or running to catch up? What might it mean to tie-in your life more closely to the rhythms of God?

● What would you see as the evidence of 'the invisible thread of grace' in your past? Should you thank God for this? Have you?

● Have you had times of having to press-on with God, even though you are passing through a desert? What strategies did you use to stay strong? What help did you get? What lessons did you learn?

● Has God given you a vision of how your future might look? Is this something you value, or could do without?

● Are you afraid of God?

■ PASSION – I will seek a connection between the deepest passions of my heart and the passion in the heart of God.

■ PLACE – I will seek to connect with God *in* the place in which I stand, *for* the place to which he is calling me.

■ PURPOSE – I will look for the connection between the evident purposes of my own life and the purposes of God for my context and culture.

■ POWER – I will seek to connect my strengths and my weaknesses to the power of God, and seek his transformation in both.

■ PROCESS – I will connect with the process and pace by which God has worked, is working and will work in my life.

■ **PERSPECTIVE – I will look for the connection between my role in the mission of God and the wider perspective of history, finding my place in God's promise-plan.**

PERSPECTIVE

Habit #6 – I will look for the connection between my role in the mission of God and the wider perspective of history, finding my place in God's promise-plan

> Why is the revelation of God at Sinai so new that it smashes all categories and idols? What exactly is so brain hammering and conscience wracking? Is it the fire, the smoke, and the thunder? These are but pyrotechnics, the merest fringe side-show, compared with the nuclear sunburst of the truth revealed – 'I am who I am.' Os Guinness[1]
>
> No problem can be solved from the same consciousness that created it. We must learn to see the world anew. Albert Einstein

EX. 3:13 *Moses said to God, 'Suppose I go to the Israelites and say to them, "The God of your fathers has sent me to you," and they ask me, "What is his name?" Then what shall I tell them?'*

14God said to Moses, 'I AM WHO I AM. This is what you are to say to the Israelites: "I AM has sent me to you."'

15God also said to Moses, 'Say to the Israelites, "The LORD, the God of your fathers – the God of Abraham, the God of Isaac and the God of Jacob – has sent me to you. This is my name for ever, the name by which I am to be remembered from generation to generation."

16'Go, assemble the elders of Israel and say to them, "The LORD, the God of your

fathers – the God of Abraham, Isaac and Jacob – appeared to me and said: I have watched over you and have seen what has been done to you in Egypt.

17And I have promised to bring you up out of your misery in Egypt into the land of the Canaanites, Hittites, Amorites, Perizzites, Hivites and Jebusites – a land flowing with milk and honey."'

In the 1960s, anthropologists had a field day with a whole series of discoveries and breakthroughs made possible by new capacities in travel and communication. In the dense jungles and remote deserts of the world, tribes were 'discovered' who had been untouched to that point by the progress of the modern world. Television audiences were thrilled to watch film recordings of stone-age tribespeople encountering their first radio, television or electric razor. The anthropologists in turn sought to learn all they could about human culture before the contact that they themselves had established swallowed up another ancient world.

One tribe studied in this way lived deep in the forest, so deep that they had always operated in an environment thick with trees and vegetation. A team of anthropologists set up a film projector and portable screen and showed them a brief sequence filmed on the plains of Africa. The film was of a vast flat landscape across which a herd of elephants were running towards the camera. The tribespeople were staggered; not only by the technology, but also by the images they saw. They were convinced that they were watching a group of very large animals growing before their eyes from tiny specks to huge monsters. At first confused by this response, the anthropologists later realised that their audience had no means of understanding visual distance. Having lived all their lives in a context in which objects were never visible more than a few metres away, they had never developed the capacity to interpret visual information on a larger scale. They had no sense of perspective.

Perspective is the capacity to understand our position in its wider context: to interpret vast distances in order to know where we stand. Without perspective, we see in two dimensions, and misinterpret the information before us. With perspective, a confused jumble of lines and shapes begins to make sense as we separate short-range, middle-range and long-range objects. Perspective allows great artists to reproduce three-dimensional objects in a two-dimensional medium, and offers magicians and illusionists the opportunity to deceive us. Programmed into computers, perspective gives us *Toy Story*, *Monsters Inc.* and *Grand Theft Auto*, and gives potentially infinite depth to a flat surface or screen. In the physical environment, perspective is essential to knowing where we are, where we've come from and where we're heading. And perspective is a vital key in our connection with the mission of God. Part of the transformation evident in the life of Moses, as he receives God's call and begins to act on it, is a change in perspective. Seeing only those things close at hand, he was moving in ever-decreasing circles, plagued by confusion and fear. Liberated to see himself in the context of God's greater plan, he was able to break the deadlock and move forward into achievement. Three-dimensional vision set him free him from the prison of self-obsession. Perspective saved him from himself. Perspective is a map of the purposes of God on which, for each of us, a huge arrow declares 'You Are Here.'

If a connection with process enables us to see the fuller picture of God's work in our lives, extending our viewfinder to take in past events and future promises,

THE EYE IN THE SKY

Imagine yourself engaging in the activities of your everyday life. Home in on an area or activity in which you have tried hard to connect with God's mission. Are you in conversation with a friend or colleague, or trying to help someone in need? Now see yourself through the lens of a camera that pulls out wider and wider from the scene. At first you can see your immediate surroundings, then the whole neighbourhood, then your town. There are lights and cars moving. Roads have become like snakes, rivers like silver ribbons. Now you are so high that the countryside surrounding your town is taken in too. Finally you see the oceans lapping at the edges of the continent on which you stand, until they too are swallowed up in the swirling mists of the earth, spinning on its axis. Now see that it is God who holds the camera, and he is smiling. How do you now feel about your place in his plans?

perspective allows us to do the same with the cosmos-spanning, planet-changing, world-reshaping mission of God. Process points us toward the depth of God's work, perspective towards its breadth. When Paul urged the Christians at Ephesus towards grasping 'how wide and long and high and deep is the love of Christ' (Eph. 3:18), he was stretching their perspective. All the passion and power in the world will not help us if we do not have the right perspective, God's perspective, on the tasks to which we are called. For Moses, connecting with God's perspective brought change in three key areas.

I Am ... *Not*

Firstly, Moses' view of God was changed. He received a new vision of the size and sovereignty of the 'I Am' God, glimpsing the creation-wide scope of God's care. The immediate focus of the Exodus story is beyond question: there is a slave people who need to be liberated, established as a nation and schooled in the laws and worship of Yahweh. But throughout the narrative there are hints of a wider view. God is not tied down to any one place or time, nor is he 'owned' by any one people. His sovereign choice of Israel as the object of his mercy means that they belong to him: but not that he belongs to them. His plans are not exhausted with their liberation: the Egyptians, too, and the nations beyond will see his glory. It is for the sake of his name – his role and reputation as the Creator of the whole earth – that God has acted as he has towards Israel. Moses trades a small-screen view of God for the wide-screen epic of a caring Creator.

Implicit in the '*I Am*' of God is a series of '*I Am Not*' statements. 'I Am Not' a local god, tied to this mountain. My power will not fade like a radio signal as you walk away from this place. 'I Am Not' one god amongst many, competing for attention in the divine population like a name on a Pokemon card. 'I Am Not' the God of the Hebrews only. Though I have called and chosen you, Egypt and the whole world will see my power also. 'I Am Not' limited in my power, like Superman frightened of exposure to green Kryptonite. There are no circumstances in which my power is diminished, other than by my choice. 'I Am Not' blind to the injustice of Pharaoh's reign, nor deaf to the cries of his victims.

For all these reasons, Moses came to see that he was not dealing with a 'god' in the Egyptian or Midianite understanding of the term. This was no pagan bullyboy, preying on the fears and superstition of local people to force offerings from them. He was not meeting with a small-time god trying hard to project an Al Capone image. This was the real thing. Whatever came of the encounter, Moses knew that his connection would be with the God of the whole earth, Maker and Sustainer of all things, Ruler of the cosmos. His father-in-law Jethro was a priest of the gods of Midian, yet no mention is made of their names or power. They are irrelevant when the real deal is in town.

Timothy Yates, in *Mission – An Invitation To God's Future*, affirms that these 'I Am Not' conditions remain true in the Christian revelation, and should dictate the shape of our mission. 'Christianity cannot be a family religion, a tribal religion, or the religion of a particular people or nation,' he writes. 'It cannot be a male religion. And it cannot be the political religion of a particular government or rule. It these religious forms develop, Christianity becomes so deformed as to be unrecognisable.'[2]

Fully committed to being part of the picture

Secondly, Moses came to see himself and his own role in the context of God's rule. He had a part to play but he was not in himself the one-stop-shop for salvation. His unfolding role as an intermediary between God and the Hebrew people exemplifies this understanding. God met with Moses one-on-one but the purpose of the encounter was much wider. It was not in Moses himself that the fruits would be seen, but in the impact on the whole people: not only in the immediate but for generations to come. Even before the liberation of the slaves, when Moses gave the people instructions for the Passover, he described them as 'a lasting ordinance for you and your descendants', and when the laws of God were given, he made a desperate plea to the people to 'teach them to your children and to their children after them.' Moses knew that he was not engaged in the work of one day or even of one lifetime – he was playing his part as a link in a chain that came from the deep past and pointed to the far future. He was, in the best sense of the phrase, a history-maker. Like a Quaker housewife embroidering her square for the community quilt, Moses saw that his

WHERE'S AARON?

Think about the sense of God's purposes that you have begun to see more clearly as you have journeyed through this book. Now ask yourself 'who has God put in place to help me?' Write down any names that come to mind. If you have an address book, go through it and underline the names of those you think can help you to connect with God's mission. Now ask yourself, 'what can I do to invest in these relationships?' 'How might this impact my priorities and time?'

small efforts would be taken up into the plans of God and would connect, somehow, with the big picture.

The late Hans Rookmaaker, professor of Art History at the Free University of Amsterdam and author of *Modern Art and the Death of a Culture*, was perhaps the twentieth century's most significant Christian commentator in his field. Having discovered in early adulthood the great truth that God's word had something to say to every area of life and culture, he 'volunteered' to take on the art world – because at the time he knew of no other Christians doing so. Well known for his deep wisdom, his short temper and his love of traditional American jazz, Rookmaaker discipled a whole generation of artists and art lovers across Europe, and was often linked with Francis and Edith Schaeffer and the L'Abri movement. He was a man who

would have an impact well beyond his own lifespan – and he knew it. Asked what motivated him to seek a Christian perspective on fine art, he would often give the same reply – 'The work that I do, I do not do for my generation, nor even for my children's generation: I do it for my children's children.'[3]

Rookmaaker understood that the Christian retreat from the art world in the nineteenth and twentieth centuries had been so extreme, and the ground to be made up was so vast, that it would take more than one professor and his students to turn it around. He knew that much of the work God had called him to involved sowing seeds, whose fruit he would never himself see. His calling and passion made sense only in the wider perspective of God's work. He had to find his place, but leave the plan to God.

From success to significance

Thirdly, Moses saw the difference perspective would make to his plans and expectations. Out-of-perspective people run the risk of viewing history as a short action movie in which they are the heroes. The plot, in this scenario, revolves around them and their role, and it is essential that all issues are resolved and all questions answered before the final credits roll. No investment can be made on which a visible return is not possible in the immediate term. No seeds can be planted whose fruit they themselves will not harvest. This is one of the key differences between being orientated towards success and towards significance. If I am looking for success, I will tend to look for it to be measured in my own lifetime. I want to see and touch and feel the fruits of my labours. If I am looking for significance, I am more likely to understand the scale on which it operates. Vincent van Gogh was never a successful artist. He died having sold only two paintings – both to his brother. But was he a significant artist? History, publishing and the auction houses of the twentieth century have resoundingly answered that question for us. Was John the Baptist a successful prophet – or a significant prophet? Was Martin Luther King Junior a successful leader, or a significant leader? A success orientation will often become more our master than our servant and drive us not into but away from true fruitfulness. An orientation towards significance takes the long-term in view, and allows us to invest in what really matters. It puts our lives into perspective.

The late Oscar Romero, Archbishop of El Salvador, expressed this need for perspective in addressing a group of priests for whom he was responsible. Ultimately martyred for speaking out for the poor and oppressed, Romero understood his own place in God's wider promise-plan. Speaking not long before his death, he said

> It helps, now and then, to step back and take the long view. The kingdom

---

FUTURE HOPE

What do you intend or expect to be doing for eternity? If you are in a group setting, think about this for a while and then tell someone else. What are the signs in your life now of this promised future?

---

is not only beyond our efforts, it is even beyond our vision. We accomplish in our lifetime only a tiny proportion of the magnificent enterprise that is God's work. Nothing we do is complete, which is another way of saying that the kingdom always lies beyond us. No statement says all that could be said. No prayer fully expresses our faith. No confession brings perfection, no pastoral visit brings wholeness. No programme accomplishes the church's mission. No set of goals and objectives achieves everything. This is what we are about. We plant seeds that one day will grow. We water seeds already planted, knowing that they hold future promise. We lay foundations that will need further development. We provide yeast that produces effects far beyond our capabilities. We cannot do everything, and there is a sense of liberation in realising this. It enables us to do something, and to do it well. It may be incomplete, but it is a beginning, a step along the way, an opportunity for the Lord's grace to enter and do the rest. We may never see the end results, but that is the difference between the master

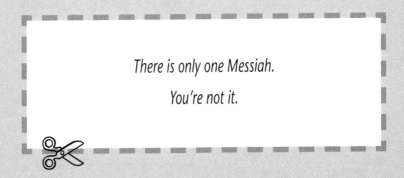

There is only one Messiah.

You're not it.

INSTRUCTIONS
Cut along dotted lines. Pin to inside of door to be visible as you leave your room or house.

builder and the worker. We are workers, not master builders; ministers not messiahs. We are prophets of a future not our own.

There are a number of things that we can do to regain God's perspective on our lives.

Telly belly – you are what you gaze upon

> You've been raised on television to believe we'll all be millionaires and movie gods and rock stars – but we won't.
>
> *Fight Club*

Firstly, we can examine just where the perspectives we now hold have come from.

In the 1970s, the United States spent some £200 million on the Apollo-Soyuz joint space link-up with the Soviet Union. When officials at NASA were asked to describe the scientific and technical benefits of the mission, they admitted there were none. The whole thing was done, they said, to provide American viewers with a space spectacular 'more thrilling than *Star Trek*.' Why would NASA invest such huge sums in a glorified publicity stunt? Because they understood the power of television to shape perspective.

Two unconnected but parallel events in the UK in recent months confirm that it is not only the USA that has become a television-shaped culture. The first is a historic legal battle in which a group of viewers will claim that the television licence fee, which funds the BBC at a cost of £112 per household, is illegal. The case is being brought before Liverpool magistrates in the context of the European Convention on Human Rights. The thirty plaintiffs – all of whom are from low-income families – claim that it is a basic human right to be able to watch television. At the same time, a survey of two hundred family doctors reveals that more and more people are getting sick as a result of television viewing. This is not a physical consequence of exposure to gamma rays but a new syndrome dubbed 'Telly Belly', in which viewers contract the same symptoms as the characters on their favourite soaps. When *Coronation Street* character Alma Sedgwick 'died' of cervical cancer, requests for smear tests went up by 200 per cent nationally. *EastEnders'* fire fighter Tom Banks, diagnosed with a brain tumour, has brought a noticeable increase in the number of patients taking their combination of headaches, suspicions and fears to their GP. More than nine out of ten of the doctors surveyed said that coverage of illness on TV, especially in the soaps, had a measurable impact on their workload. Television has become so much a part of the fabric of our lives that the distinctions are blurred between on-screen and off-screen realities. Not only that, but the notion of life without TV is seen as an extreme form of poverty, amounting to a loss of basic human rights.

These stories are not cited here as ammunition in an anti-television sermon. They are here to illustrate a principle as old as Moses – that which you gaze upon shapes you. The small screen is just one example of the 'perspective-shaping' forces in our culture. Print advertising also has significant power, as do the aural messages of the music and radio industries. I found out recently that more money is spent in the UK each year on adverts prepared for radio than on those made for TV: what you hear, as much as what you watch, will shape you. The repeated commands in the Old Testament against idolatry are in part founded on this reality. Focus your eyes on idols, give them your attention and adulation and you will find yourself becoming like them. Focus on Yahweh, and the same will be true. Your focal point changes your perspective, and thereby alters your expectations and intentions.

Many of us fear that our perspective is too big a thing to change. How can we alter the whole way we see the world? The truth is that we can, by rooting ourselves in truth; by taking time to look and learn – by gazing on the God who has saved us. Reading; study; worship; prayer; contemplation; silence; conversation – all these have their place in the fight to stay focused. The primary thrust of the traditional 'spiritual disciplines' of the Christian faith is to ground us in God's

SPIRITUAL DISCIPLINES

How much do you know about the traditional 'spiritual disciplines' of the Christian faith? There is a strong link between the practise of these and the discernment of the plans and purposes of God. If you have never read Richard Foster's *Celebration of Discipline*, try to get hold of a copy and set aside three months to work through it. If you have read it already, find your copy and review it. How might you introduce, or re-introduce, the disciplines to your life?[4]

perspective. We see ourselves *in* his eyes and our world *through* his eyes.

There is a simple question you can use as a means of assessing your own perspectives. It is this: 'What do your eyes and ears spend the most time doing?' Whatever the answer, your heart will not be far behind.

My glorious – bigger than the air I breathe

What is our life on earth, if not discovering, becoming conscious of, penetrating, contemplating, accepting, loving this mystery of God, the unique reality which surrounds us, and in which we are immersed like meteorites in space?

Carlo Carretto[5]

Secondly, we can work at broadening our picture of God's mission.

God had to challenge Moses, time and time again, to broaden his perspective: just as he did in every subsequent generation in Israel. The temptation was always to see God's 'election' of Israel as the full and final statement of his plans. God has chosen us, and it's enough. But even in the Exodus narrative itself, this view is challenged. God's deliverance of Israel is not an end in itself but a means towards the display of his greater glory. It is for the whole earth and for the sake of his name as its Maker. God has his sights set on the all the nations, even as he is choosing one nation to serve him.

There is an ancient Hasidic story told of a great celebration in heaven after the Israelites are delivered from the Egyptians at the Red Sea, and the Egyptian armies are drowned. The angels are cheering and dancing, thrilled at God's great victory. Everyone in heaven is full of joy. Then one of the angels notices that God hasn't joined the party. He asks the archangel Michael, 'Where is God? Why isn't God here celebrating?' And Michael answers, 'God is not here because he is off by himself weeping. You see, many thousands of his children were drowned today.'

Do you have a view of salvation that works for you but has little to say to others? Is your God available only to those of your colour and culture? Do you serve a tribal god, or the God of the whole earth?

Robert Webber is an evangelical scholar in the United States who has made this journey for himself in recent years. Long established in an understanding of salvation as personal, he has more recently broadened his view to take in the whole of Christ's victory – like a camera switched to 'panoramic mode'. He explains

> In the Christian faith the key to the puzzle is the work of Jesus Christ. Once we have a solid grasp of the meaning of his work, the rest of the faith falls together around it. As far back as I can remember I was told that Christ was central to the Christian faith. However, when I began to reflect on the teaching I had received, I realised that the importance of Christ was always explained in terms of my personal salvation, little more. I have come to see through the study of the early Christian tradition that my view of Christ was severely limited. It wasn't that I didn't believe rightly. I simply didn't understand how far-reaching and all-inclusive Christ really was. When I discovered the universal and cosmic nature of Christ, I was given the key to a Christian way of viewing the whole world, a key that unlocked the door to a rich storehouse of spiritual treasures.[6]

Two million short – getting perspective on lifestyle

Lead us from the unreal
To the real.
Lead us from darkness
To light.
Lead us from death
To immortality.

A prayer from India

Thirdly, we can seek a life and lifestyle that is built on a God-given perspective.

A story reported in one of New York's leading papers featured an interview with the wife of a baseball player who had made his name with the New York Yankees. One of the undisputed stars of the team, this man had just had his contract renewed in a deal worth eighty-nine million dollars. In the negotiations leading up to the deal, he refused for some time to sign. A rival team had offered him ninety-one million dollars, and he was hoping that the Yankees would match the offer. But they wouldn't budge. Eighty-nine million dollars was their highest offer, and in the end he signed. Describing her feelings on the day he came home with the news, his wife said, 'When I saw him walk in the house, I immediately knew that he had not succeeded in persuading them to move up from eighty-nine to ninety-one million. He felt so rejected. It was one of the saddest days of our lives.'

If we lose God's perspective on our lives, we will make decisions built on false expectations and unreal hopes. More often than not, we will overplay our own importance, overstate our own rights and overestimate our own needs. The importance, rights and needs of others, by contrast, we will fail to see. Only a re-orientation of our lives around God's perspective will save us from these distortions. The paintings of Marc Chagall are full of passion and colour, capturing on canvas the vibrancy of life in Paris in the early twentieth century. His subjects were often drawn from dream sequences, with people and symbols floating in fantasy settings. But his ultimate source was always the real world. Describing the process by which he judged the worth of a painting, he said 'When I am finishing a picture I hold some God-made object up to it – a rock, a flower, the branch of a tree or my hand – as a kind of final test. If the painting stands up beside a thing man cannot make, the painting is authentic. If there's a clash between the two, it is bad art.' Chagall knew that the quality of his

FIRST STEPS

What is there on the far horizon of God's promises, plans and purposes for your life that you can take one small step towards right now: before the end of this week? Decode what that step will be, no matter how small, and commit to taking it. Write it down.

work could only ever be judged against a true perspective: in his case the witness of nature.

What is the perspective against which you judge the decisions you are making and the lifestyle you enjoy? Is there a 'big picture' of the mission of God that might help you towards a more realistic assessment? Three questions may help you:

- How does the decision I am taking affect the reputation of God in the world?

- Where are the poor in my thinking about this decision?

- Is my 'self' a huge presence at the centre of this choice, or simply one consideration amongst others?

Getting our lives in perspective means appreciating, exploring, enjoying and engaging with all that God is doing in the world. How much do you see of the panorama of God's mission? How often are you aware of God at work? How often are you able to hold up your own choices against a picture of the mission of God? When you do, how authentic do your life-choices seem?

Songwriter Matt Redman has commented recently on the results of holding up his own perspectives and choices against God's deeper and wider mission, in the particular context of leading public worship. 'I've been challenged on this a lot recently,' he writes, 'I say I'm a worship

---

COVER STORY

Take a look at the image on the cover of this book. In your mind, allocate one electrical pin to each of the Six Habits we have explored. Passion, Place, Purpose, Power, Process and Perspective. If this plug were your connection, which of the six would be weak or mis-wired?

---

leader, and I also say that worship is far more than just about music. So why are all my acts of worship leading done through music? When it comes to reaching the broken of this world, why am I so often near the back of the queue? I'm longing to be a worshipper who sets an example for others to follow, not just with my lips, but with my life.'[7]

Unless you connect with God's perspective, it is unlikely that you will sustain for long a connection with his purposes or power. Your own aspirations and expectations, and the messages that plague your ears and eyes, will act like magnets pulling at your inner compass. You will struggle to value the call of God unless his value system is your framework. You will fail to see the hollowness of other callings unless the solid ore of his mission is your True North. If it has been a struggle for you to connect with God's purposes and power, try taking some time out to refresh your connection with his perspective. Train your eyes to follow where he leads, and let your heart come tumbling after.

PERSPECTIVE applied

Use these six questions to explore the dynamic of 'perspective' in your own life. Where do you see yourself in relation to the wider picture of God's purposes, promises and plans?

● Think of the 'macro' picture of God's mission as the wide-screen view, taking in the broad panorama of all that God has done, is doing and will do to redeem the cosmos, and think of the 'micro' view as the small-screen picture of your part in the plan. Which picture is clearer for you? What steps can you take to bring clarity to the other picture?

● Tim Jeffrey and Steve Chalke, in *Connect!*, suggest that the destiny of the church in the twenty-first century is 'to be Global Christians, part of a Global Church working together on God's Global Mission.'[8] Do you agree? What does this imply for you?

● What are the things that distort your perspective? Is money a strong influence on you? What else distracts and misguides you? What can you do to lessen these negative influences?

● If God spoke to you in an audible voice, what accent do you think he might have?

● If you are a link in a chain of God's purposes – who are you connected to? Where are the relationships that are significant to your participation in the plans of God? Have you invested in these connections? Could you?

● Many people focus on too narrow a definition of God's mission – it is just about people being converted, or just about feeding the poor. If God's mission is bigger and wider than you thought it was, what is it that you have missed? Imagine the mission of God as an ocean view. What do you see at the furthest visible point? What is in the middle distance? What do you see close at hand?

1 Os Guinness, *The Call*, p65

2 Timothy Yates, Ed., *Mission: An Invitation to God's Future* (Sheffield: Cliff College, 2000)

3 Hans Rookmaaker, *Modern Art and the Death of a Culture*

4 Richard Foster, *Celebration of Discipline* (Harper and Row, 1990)

5 Carlo Carretto, *Letters from the Desert* (Orbis books, 1982)

6 Robert Webber, *Ancient Future Faith: Evangelicalism for a Postmodern world* (Baker Book House, 1999), p39, 43

7 Matt Redman, *The Unquenchable Worshipper* (Kingsway, 2001)

8 Steve Chalke and Tim Jeffrey, *Connect!*, (Carlisle: Spring Harvest Publishing, 2003)

EPILOGUE

Make and Maintain the Connection

Passion, Place, Purpose, Power, Process and Perspective: these are the six 'pins' that will help you to find your connection with God's mission. It should be clear by now that this is no instant achievement but the work of a lifetime. No one can ever say, in any final sense, that they have 'made the connection' – only that they are more connected then they were.

My Windows XP operating system has a new feature called 'System Restore'. This enables me to select specific moments at which to take a 'snapshot' of my computer's memory allocations and system settings. If things go badly wrong at some stage in the future (it will always be three o'clock in the morning, and I will have just seen a dialogue box that says 'Are you quite sure you want to do this?' and foolishly clicked the YES button) I can get back to where I was. The computer is able to make a comparison between its current state and that of two weeks or two months ago.

How would you fare if 'System Restore Points' were established in your life? If you look back, say, to a point twelve months ago, how does your current state compare?

- Are you more or less passionate about God's call on your life? Are you hearing and seeing more or less of his passion in your everyday world?

- Is your sense of the presence of God in the place in which you stand, and of the promise of God for the place to which he is calling you, stronger or weaker than one year ago?

- Is your picture of the purpose of God for your life sharper or more blurred than it was twelve months ago? Have you edged closer to God's purposes, or have the decisions you have made pulled you further away?

- Are you more dependent on God's power than you were, or less so?

- Has your awareness of the 'invisible thread of grace' in your past grown or diminished? Do you feel less trapped by past events and the habits they have made in you – or more so?

What of your future – are your far horizons more or less substantial in your thoughts?

■ Is your life and lifestyle more shaped by God's 'widescreen' perspective now than it was, or less so? Has your vision of God's mission grown wider or narrower? Of the key decisions you have taken in the past twelve months – purchases, career developments, life choices – how many have reflected God's perspective and brought you further into his plans?

The purpose of these questions is to demonstrate that your goal is movement, not arrival. It is the direction you are travelling in that matters – no matter how small the advances you have made. Taking some time to explore these questions can help you in two ways.

Firstly, it can give you a 'global view' of your connection to God's mission. If all or nearly all your responses are negative, you face the challenge that you are slipping away from God's purposes instead of creeping towards them. The realities of Christian growth are such that the majority of people who drift away from God's purposes do so in a series of small, almost imperceptible steps. Equally, those who embrace God's purposes for their lives usually do so as the result of a whole series of choices and changes, many of them covering very little ground. If the majority of your answers are positive you have, at the very least, the assurance that

there is forward movement in your life. It may be slower than you had hoped, and there may be patches of disappointment – but the evidence of progress is there.

There is a graphic and dramatic scene in the oldest Disney version of the Snow White story. The handsome Prince has found his way to the castle in which the sleeping Princess lies. He has only to kiss her to gain eternal bliss. But before he can do so he must cut his way through the twisting and terrifying jungle of thorns that has grown around the castle walls. Our hero unsheathes his sword and hacks away at the tangle of thorn branches, many as thick as his own arms. The going is hard, but he is determined, and in time he breaks through. Picture your life in these terms. In the castle there lies, sleeping, the immeasurable promise of your life taken up into the purposes of God. All you need to do is to make the connection. But to get there, you must hack away at the thorns. Ask yourself – 'How am I doing?' Are you closer to your goal than you were, or have you dropped back? Take up your sword. Hack away.

Secondly, your answers to these questions might tell you where the thorns are at their thickest. If you have been able to answer positively in a number of areas, but are taken aback by your negativity in other areas, this may tell you where to concentrate your efforts. Reflect on the areas in your journey through the 'Six Habits' that have seemed to you like doorways you might go through.

Go back to these areas and spend some time in reflection. Hold the data of your life up against any insights you have gained into the workings of the purposes of God. Identify any specific action that suggest themselves – and think about when, where and how you might take these steps.

As I have worked through this 'System Restore' exercise for myself, I have seen areas both of progress and of frustration. My passion for the purposes of God is undimmed, and my sense of his plans for my life is stronger now than it was twelve months ago. I feel that several particularly heavy thorns have been cut away. But I am also aware, as I reflect on process and perspective, that I am hindered by habits formed deeply in me by events and influences in my past. I can see quite clearly that there are three or four areas in which I need to identify and deal with these thorns. I have also come to see in recent months that many of my choices and decisions have my 'self' very largely set in their centre. For all the rhetoric of seeking to serve God, I know that I am often guilty of self-seeking, and am genuinely afraid of the personal discomfort that selfless decisions might bring. This is not all that I see as I consider my recent life in the light of the 'Six Habits' framework – but it is enough to illustrate the extent to which our responses to the different questions can vary: and my answers do point me towards a prescription for change. At least in part, I know what some of the steps I can take in the coming months are, and my confidence is boosted

---

NEXT STEPS

Write down some of your thoughts and feelings as you have read this book. Note any dreams and visions that have come to you, any old promises you have been reminded of or any good intentions that you have come back to. Put what you have written in an envelope and address it to yourself. Ask a friend to post it one year from today.

---

that I will be able to say, twelve months hence, that I am more connected than I was to God's mission.

Vine is the kingdom

There is a helpful parallel to the call of Moses in the New Testament, when Jesus describes those who will follow him as branches of a vine. In a much-quoted passage in John 15:1-8, Jesus says 'I am the vine; you are the branches', and explores in some depth just what this image might mean. At the heart of the passage are two repeated commands – 'remain in me' and 'go and bear fruit'. The precise wording varies with different sentence structures, but all together the idea of 'remaining' is mentioned eight times in the course of eight verses, while fruit and fruitfulness turn up seven times.

What is not immediately apparent, but becomes so when you think more carefully about the way vines grow, is the dynamic tension between these two commands. In effect they call for two equal and opposite movements.

'Remaining' is about staying close to the root. It calls us to hold tight to the source; to draw strength from him; to face inwards and give attention to our own nurture and growth. 'Remain in me' is a call to come in. 'Go and bear fruit', by contrast, is a call to go out. The best fruits on a vine do not grow near the root, but out at the very tips of the branches, where the plant is pushing out into the oxygen and sunlight. Fruit that grows too close to the root is often spoiled. While there is force pulling the branches into the root, holding them tight and keeping them connected, there is a force of life pushing them out. The vine is a particular type of plant that pushes out. Vineyard growers will set out long fence-like wire structures to allow the vine to grow at full stretch. For health and growth, a vine needs to push outwards.

The picture Jesus gives establishes these two equal and opposite forces. We are pulled in to Christ; feeding on him; drawing strength; seeing our minds and hearts transformed; facing inwards to the full flood of his nurturing love. But we are also thrust out into our world; pushed to where the fruit will come; taut along the wires of God's purposes. Our connection to the mission of God is kept alive by the tension of these two. We are stretched between nurture and purpose; between gaining and giving; between the inward focus of renewal and the outward focus of redemption. This is why it is impossible to say whether salvation is primarily an inward or an outward movement. It is both. Likewise, forgiveness is neither a matter of simply receiving nor of simply offering – it is a complex weaving together of the two. Is the shalom of God something you take in, or something you give out? Yes.

- Is your connection with the passion, purpose and power of God for your benefit? Yes.

- Is it for the benefit of others? Yes again.

- Are the processes of God's work in your life aimed at changing you? Yes.

- Are they aimed at changing the world? Yes again, again.

It is impossible to separate the inward and outward dimensions of God's connections into our lives. We are called both to remain and to bear fruit; both to stay and to go. We are both priests and prophets, both Martha and Mary; both Peter and Paul. If we focus only on remaining, there is no fruit. Spend too much time facing inwards and you will soon see that nothing changes in your world. If we focus only on fruit-bearing, looking outward with no thought of our own health, there is still no fruit. To be connected to your culture on the one hand, but disconnected from your God on the other, is no gain. Empty activism and bland relevance are equally of no value.

No matter how deeply you immerse yourself in the culture to which you feel called, it is crucial that you keep your connection to Christ. No matter how deeply you immerse yourself in Christ, it is crucial that you keep your connection to the culture to which you are called.

This is the place God has appointed for us, in the now-but-not-yet of his promise-plan. We are stretched between the certainty of redemption and the reality of the fall. Our lives are shaped by the promises of God and by the presence of evil. We are strong and weak; compliant and defiant; called and cowardly. Like Moses, we are caught up in the rushing wind of God's purposes but caught up, too, in our own small minds. We struggle to find our feet on the shifting sands of our age, and we struggle to place our hand in the hand of God. But here is the whisper of God to us – 'You can connect.' This is the miracle of our faith, that it is possible – with all our weakness and failings; in a hostile and unhelpful culture; trapped as we are by the habits of the past; driven as we are by appetites and the need for comfort; frightened as we are of stepping out – to connect with our Creator. It is possible, even in the chaos of our age, to plug in to God's purposes, and to know that our lives are centred on a plan that is not ours – scored to a music we have not written.

This is the miracle of all miracles. God has a plan, and you have a part in it. Connect. Find your place. Connection is the life that you were made for.

Equipping Christians to live actively, biblically and wholeheartedly for Christ — that's the goal of all that Spring Harvest does.

The Main Event

The largest Christian event of its kind in Europe — an Easter-time gathering of over 60,000 people for learning, worship and fun. The programme includes varied and inspiring choices for everyone, no matter how old or young, and no matter where you are in your Christian life.

Resources

- *Books* to help you understand issues that matter — prayer, family issues, Bible themes, workplace and more
- *Music albums* introducing new songs and showcasing live worship from the Main Event each year
- *Childrens resources* including popular music albums and songbooks
- *Songbooks* to introduce the best new worship material each year
- *Audio tapes* of teaching from Spring Harvest — a selection of thousands is available to choose from
- *Youth pastoral resources, songwords projection software, video services and more...*

Conferences

- *Youthwork the conference* — for volunteer youth workers, run in partnership with Youthwork magazine, YFC, Oasis Youth Action and the Salvation Army
- *At Work Together* to equip workers to effectively live and witness for Christ in today's challenging workplace.

Le Pas Opton is a beautiful four star holiday site on the French Vendée coast, exclusively owned and operated by Spring Harvest. Mobile homes, tents or your own tent/tourer — take your choice at this delightful resort where you'll find top quality facilities and excellent service.

Our aim at *Le Pas Opton* is to give you the opportunity for relaxation and refreshment of body, mind and spirit. Call Spring Harvest Holidays on 0870 060 3322 for a free brochure.

INVESTOR IN PEOPLE

For more information contact our Customer Service team on 01825 769000 or visit our website at www.springharvest.org

Spring Harvest. A Registered Charity.